All the
Silent
Spaces

All the Silent Spaces

a memoir

Christine Ristaino

She Writes Press

Published 2019
Printed in the United States of America
ISBN: 978-1-63152-569-8 pbk
ISBN: 978-1-63152-570-4 ebk
Library of Congress Control Number: 2019931206

For information, address:
She Writes Press
1569 Solano Ave #546
Berkeley, CA 94707

Interior design by Tabitha Lahr

She Writes Press is a division of SparkPoint Studio, LLC.

Please note: all names and some details in this book have been changed to protect the identities of the real people I have written about.

I dedicate this book to my children, Maddy and Benny, to my husband, Christopher, to my parents and brothers, Carl, Jean, Carl, Phil, Andy, and Mark, to my nieces and nephews, Margaret, Isabella, Dylan, Carter, and Harley, to my inspirational students, and to Isabel for all the late-night talks that led me to this moment.

Contents

Introduction: Ten Year Anniversary

It has been ten years since the event that inspired this book
occurred on a black pavement,
a bloodied woman lying in a parking lot
while her children stared and sobbed.

Since then,
the world has changed.
It's more fractured,
more united in hidden, unspoken truths
of a look, a shiver, a hope, a touch.

Now, more than ever,
we need to engage with difficult topics,
reach out to others,
listen to each other in a sea of uncertainty,
sit together with the experiences we share,
and find common ground.

It is my hope
this book will create space
for difficult conversations,
for bearing witness to each other's stories,
so we will be less alone in them;
stories owned and shouldered by the world,
not just each of us, alone.

Now more than ever we need this.
More than ever we are called to take chances with our voices,
so tied as we are to each other in our shared fluency of experience.

Retrogression Defined

ret·ro·gres·sion
noun
1. the act of retrogressing; movement backward.
2. Biology. degeneration; retrograde metamorphosis; passing
from a more complex to a simpler structure.
dictionary.reference.com/browse/retrogression

Prologue

The shopping cart we find in the parking lot has Cinderella on it and my children think they are at Disneyland. Their chubby arms and legs move with purpose as they climb inside. As I push my children toward the store, I glance down at them. They're cute. I know this about my kids. My curly hair blows in the breeze, lifting and settling every few seconds near the sides of my face. When I reach the sidewalk and the wheels become stuck on the curb, a man on a bench stands and walks in our direction. I see him and acknowledge him with a nod, hoping he'll help me lift the cart onto the sidewalk.

The man grabs the shopping cart with one hand and with the other he throws his fist into my face. The pain concentrates on the bridge of my nose for a second and then moves into my head. I can feel something open inside me. I smell blood as it flows out my nose.

The man is wiry. I keep my hands on the cart, wanting to create space underneath for my children, who are somewhere below me.

Something isn't right with my shoulder. All the ligaments, muscles, and skin are pulling off the bone and the bone itself seems to move away from the socket. Each time it is pulled, I feel a wave of nausea. I want to crouch low to the ground and nurse my arm, but my children are below. I squeeze the cart, almost touching my palms to my fingers.

I stare at the man's face. It is angular, thin. It does not smile. The lips press themselves together, wormy, contemptuous. I hear a crack. It sounds like the snap of a chicken bone. This time it's my jaw. The force brings my head back. My neck hits my shoulders. Another wave of nausea, and something wirelike pulls against my arm. It's my purse strap. It must be caught on the cart. I thrust my shoulder back to keep it in place, and this brings on searing pain.

He moves closer. His breath is sour. There's blood on his face and hand. He tries to yank my purse from me. So that's what this is about.

"You're a prick," I say and his eyes move away from mine.

He steps back and then his fist strikes my right eye. I am retching. The muscles in both arms ache with this new force. I let go of the cart and cover my face with my hands. The purse strap slides off my shoulder. I'm falling. There's the thud of my own head and a sharp pain where it hits the pavement. Dots appear and disappear in front of me—an electrical current, the wiring all wrong. Blood creeps through the cracks in my hands, and then I hear his footsteps as they recede, and look to see my two children inches away, staring from the princess cart. I can feel the cold blacktop on my skin. I hear a child wailing. It's my daughter. I am covered in my own blood. I want to close my eyes.

Retrogression 1:
September 17, 2007, 2:30 p.m.

It is the Monday after the attack. I am at a meeting with the second highest ranking official at my university, Provost Ray Stevens, a historian by training, a gentle speaker, a black man. He is talking about a trip he has recently taken and I can't remember where he went, even though he must have told us three times. It is a rare and important meeting, for we are finalizing something that will change the university in a positive way, but they are asking me about my black eye, or something about my eyes. "Why won't the health center give you an appointment for a scan?" they ask. "Because they didn't have one available until Thursday." Suddenly Provost Stevens is on the phone and I am in a car, driving there, driving to the health center with an appointment, just like that, only I am not driving; my colleague Jackie is. Then I am at the hospital. "Why did you take me here?" I ask her. "Because your pupils were two different sizes and you were slurring your words," she says. I don't care. I want to hear more about Jackie's crazy childhood with eleven kids, or something like that, playing on the train tracks and sneaking into movie theaters.

Chapter 1: Victims

I have heard stories from victims since my late teens. Initially I listened, but never knew how to react. When a man beat me up at the store in front of my children, stories of survival became part of who I was. Overnight, I was a member of a community. Stories tumbled into my pathway, one after another.

Zahra called me immediately after she was attacked when I was living in Seattle in my early twenties. She was badly beaten, with a black eye, a sprained ankle, a dislocated knee, and gashes to her head. I walked through her front door into the middle of a conversation.

"All I hear is you apologizing for this guy. You have to call the police," her boyfriend said.

"No, I can't. I promised I wouldn't."

"But he could hurt somebody else," he told her.

"No, I absolutely cannot," she said.

Zahra had been walking her dogs in the park when a man jumped her under an overpass. He grabbed her hair and smashed her head backward into a concrete wall. Then he threw her down and pinned her to the ground.

"I am going to rape you and kill you," he told her.

Zahra began to say her name, first to herself and then to him.

"I'm Zahra. I work at the university. I'm innocent. Who are you?"

"Joe," he finally said. "My name's Joe."

Joe pushed himself off Zahra's body. Zahra managed to stand and take Joe's hand.

"Joe," she said. "You are innocent. God loves you. I need you to help me collect my dogs and then walk me to my car."

Joe began to sob and threw his arms around Zahra's legs. Zahra was an atheist, but she began to pray, "Dear God, please forgive Joe."

By the time they arrived at Zahra's car, they had formed a bond.

"I will not call the police if you promise not to do this again, to anybody," Zahra said.

"I won't," Joe promised.

Around this same time, Natalie, a college friend of mine teaching nearby, called to warn me she would be on the six o'clock news. During an assembly at her high school, a student had grabbed her around the neck and placed a knife to her throat.

"We're up next," he told her.

He dragged her out to the middle of the basketball court, and everyone laughed until they realized he was serious.

He took the microphone. "I'm going to kill her, and I'm the one you'll all remember," he said. He repeated these same words a second time.

Natalie tried to escape his grasp by tucking her chin and pushing her arms up over her head. As she did this, the school principal snuck behind her attacker and grabbed the knife. The only injury was a cut on the principal's hand.

People sent Natalie bouquets of flowers, and she got a few days off. Then she went back to work. Teachers at her school thought Natalie must have been failing her student, but this wasn't true. There was actually trust between the two. "He was doing fine in my class. It's a power thing," Natalie told me. "Until communities can help children to fully become themselves, this type of crime will continue to happen."

Margo, a neighbor, invited me to coffee right after I was beaten up. She told me how difficult it was to get over an assault and described what had happened to her. The man was in his early twenties, and Margo remembers being annoyed when he tried to coax her friend into staying with him at a party. She was waiting in the car when she saw the man hit her friend in the face. Margo shot out of the front seat and confronted him. The man hit Margo and knocked her over. She landed in the dirt, muddied and confused.

Later that evening, Margo called her mom from her friend's house, sobbing. "Please come and pick me up. Something's happened," she said.

The people in Margo's town wanted her to write it all off as an unfortunate peculiarity of the man's character. He had a reputation for assaulting women. "These are just the actions of a drunk man," they told her. "Let it go."

But Margo and her mother wouldn't let it go.

A court battle ensued, humiliating and long, but it felt right. He was convicted of assault. Margo went off to college the following year and no longer visits her hometown.

A year after my own attack I met Marina at a university workshop. Marina asked me which courses I had been teaching and if I was happy to be finished with the semester. I responded that I had just completed a leave of absence.

"Were you doing research?" she asked.

"No," I said, and I began outlining the circumstances of my leave: how my children had seen me bleeding on the pavement, how my son could no longer sleep at night, how my daughter had cried every night before bed for a month. I told her I was writing about it. Then she told me her story.

"I worked at a bank until the day we were robbed. They had us lie on the floor. They all had guns. I was the bank's one black employee. They took everyone's money from their drawers except mine. My drawer counted down perfectly, to the penny. Maybe it was a togetherness kind of thing. I don't know. But hey, I didn't want that kind of togetherness. Afterward, my employers and the police thought I had something to do with it. I never went back to the bank. For a while, every time I saw somebody with a nylon coat and one of those ski caps, I would get nervous. But I had to get over that fast. I couldn't be afraid of my brothers."

"You said your children were afraid after your attack?" Marina asked after a pause.

"Sam was for a while. Every time we went to his preschool and a black dad dropped off his son, Sam would crawl behind my legs and hide."

"You know, my brother was jumped by three guys, but my mother didn't want him to press charges. She went and talked with the attackers' mothers instead. 'That would have more of a positive effect,' she had said, and it was good for me to see as a child. My mother explained she didn't want them to go through the criminal justice system. It would destroy them. It would turn them into criminals. I'm glad she gave me this perspective. My father was upset. He wanted them all to be in jail."

"My husband, too," I said. "He's so angry. After I was robbed, he called my cell phone, and somebody answered. My husband yelled into the phone, 'Do you like to beat up women and scare children? Do you get your kicks this way, you asshole?' My children and I have all had counseling. But Mark is still fuming mad."

"This must be more difficult for your husband right now. The three of you experienced it together, but your husband, he was alone in this, wondering what to do."

I nodded, and we walked silently.

I thought of Marina's story, and the others flowed to the surface—Zahra's near-death escape, Natalie's knife-wielding student, Margo's court case, and many more. Two friends were molested as children. Male and female friends were beaten up for things they said or did at school. A friend who worked at an Atlanta bar lost control of his bladder when two men put a gun to his head.

And there were more incidents that came to mind. A woman I knew was raped in the 1950s when she was only thirteen. My college roommate was mugged on a dark street in Berkeley. My brother was beaten up numerous times for his wallet in San Francisco. Another brother was held up on a New York subway. Two friends were threatened at gunpoint in their home in Atlanta. My own grandmother received a black eye on more than one occasion from my grandfather. And my brother George was robbed at gunpoint when he worked at a sub shop. Even I had been raped when I was in college, held down by arms much larger than mine, paralyzed by the weight of his body as he forced his way into me. And there was one event I had kept to myself for years: a man I trusted had molested me when I was nine. I hid this story, even from myself. It barely affected me, I reasoned, and like other events I had heard about, I felt distant from them all. But more than twenty years later, in a parking lot, seeing my children's faces during our attack had jolted me awake.

Retrogression 2:
September 16, 2007, 11:30 a.m.

The grant writer from work visits me at home. She is com-
passionate and nervous at the same time. "Make sure you do
something about this. Take some time off. Your eye looks like
it hurts. What can I do to help you?" We have been working
on a grant. It's due in a few days, and I can tell she doesn't want
to be stuck finishing it. "Let me know if there's anything I can
do for you. I'm not sure how to send in the grant. I'm going to
need help with that part," she says. I don't say anything.

Chapter 2: Separated

"Molested" is the wrong word. It gives the impression you are being bothered at a cookout by a pesky fly. The word I would use instead is "separated" because something of this nature separates you from family, from friends, from your feelings, from yourself.

A few days after writing the pages in the previous chapter, I reread "Victims" and am startled by my admission that I was molested. I cringe as I imagine my parents reading it one day and hide the story deep in a folder on my desk. But the word remains on the page, as persistent as a fly.

Retrogression 3:
September 15, 2007, 11:40 p.m.

My husband and I drink tea. "Are you okay?" he asks. "Yes," I say. We discuss Ada's sobs, and Sam's smooth little hand stroking the side of my face. We talk about Donna, her chance visit to the store, Louise's passionate run from her car, and how comforting her presence was. We are amazed at how articulate the children were when they recounted the event. Louise, Donna, and Olivia, my sister-in-law who arrived later, said exactly what needed to be said to calm them. And what about the couple too shocked to help, and the stranger who threw her arms around me? When everything is said that needs to be said, we put our mugs in the sink, turn off the lights, and go to bed.

Chapter 3: Reverend Conversations

May we have the courage to reject retaliation and vengeance.

....

And a willingness to listen beyond the harshness
To what's really going on

....

Weaving webs of listening
Weaving webs of repair and restoration.

—Excerpts from a poem on violence read on September 16, 2007, in Atlanta, Georgia, by Reverend John Phillip

I had never visited a minister before. The ministers of my past had always seemed unapproachable, their beliefs so distant from mine. They were the priests my mother visited and quoted. "Yes" to life, "no" to gay marriage, "no" to birth control, "no" to women priests. Even when I was young, I felt like an imposter in those high-ceilinged buildings.

Nobody should charge my car, I thought as I put it into park.

"Thank you," I said as he shut my son's door, my face still flushed. "Thank you," I said again.

I put my hand on my chest, felt the strong, strong beat there, and slowly put my car into drive.

Retrogression 4:
September 15, 2007, 11:35 p.m.

My husband makes tea. He places two tea bags into wide mugs and waits for the whistle. Then he pours hot water over the bags to steep. He carries the mugs into the living room, places them on the coffee table, and sits next to me, putting a hand on my knee.

Chapter 4: Interrogations

"What did he look like?" "Was he black?" "Where is he now, in jail?" "Do you think he was on drugs?" "What was he wearing?" "Maybe he's from the Million Dollar Corner. Do you think he's from there?"

The day after we were attacked, my cells began the work of rebuilding, reinforcing, reconnecting tissue. First the bruises on my face would turn yellow and brown and then fade away. Next, the muscles in my arms would lose their soreness. Soon I would get used to the constant tingling that was to take residence in my lips. I would have physical therapy on my jaw for months after the attack. Later, I would have a bubble in my eye removed, a liquid-filled clear thing that had formed after a direct hit in the face. Slowly, I would feel comfortable again in public places. One day I would take my children to a store and we wouldn't talk about being attacked as we held hands and ran toward safety.

During the days that followed, neighbors, friends, and relatives all seemed to speak a language that neither I nor those closest to me would decode for months. My husband, children, parents, and brothers were the only people whose rhythms and language synced with mine, and when I was not near them, I craved their silent support.

"I was attacked," I told Ricky when I ran into him in a checkout line with a black eye. "Just a week ago I was at a friend's fortieth birthday party, not a care in the world. Then two days ago, the kids and I are at a store and . . ."

"A black man?" Ricky asked. "Was he black?"

"What are you saying?" I asked as I pulled up the hood of my jacket and prepared to leave.

"I'm sorry, Christine. I'm not being racist if that's what you're getting at. I was just curious."

"Well, you could have asked me about the kids or something."

"Are they okay?"

"Yes," I said.

"Good. I hope you're better. It looks like he got you pretty good in that eye. Hey, I'll call you."

"I cried all day and all night about this," my mother said. "The next morning I went to work, a zombie. But when I told my colleagues, all they could say was what they would do differently. 'I wouldn't get mugged because I walk fast to my car and look from side to side.' 'When I walk out of stores, I hold on to my bag like a weapon and I am on guard.' 'Me, too. I hold my keys in between my fingers and I'm ready to punch someone. This would never happen to me.' Christine, they seemed to ignore one thing: that my daughter had been attacked and it wasn't her fault. They didn't want to admit this could happen to them."

The barrage of questions about my attacker lasted days. "What does it matter?" I said to neighbors, friends, my beloved uncle. They didn't recognize me anymore.

"Why do they have to ask these questions?" I asked my friend Don as we walked out of the Unitarian congregation followed by our children. "Don't they care about me, how I'm doing? What if I had fallen off a cliff? Would the first question they asked be about the scenery? About the Million Dollar Corner? What the hell is that anyway?"

"They love you. We all care about you. They just want to know who they need to be afraid of," he responded. "You haven't heard of the Million Dollar Corner?" he added, smiling. "It's one of the roughest corners of Atlanta. They sell about a million dollars worth of drugs there a year."

"Well, he was black. The police will never catch him, and I don't think they even cared to look for him. And why would he be chasing my twenty dollars in a parking lot if he could stand on the Million Dollar Corner and sell drugs? So I guess he's not from there."

We both laughed and then glanced around to account for our children, who took turns rolling down a small hill in front of the parking lot.

"Besides, this was just one man," I said. "How can one man prove or disprove anything?"

"They're all afraid," Don said. "Already nobody feels safe, and then you are beaten up and our whole existence is in question. Why do we want to know who to be afraid of? Because maybe, just maybe if we know, we won't be attacked in front of our children at a store."

Retrogression 5:
September 15, 2007, 11:15 p.m.

When we are all safely inside, door closed and locked, my husband does the only thing he can do at a time like this. He calls the locksmith and puts the children to bed. He phones the credit card companies. When all the practical details have been taken care of, he stands by the stove and waits for the teakettle to whistle.

Chapter 5: Homeward Bound

L ess than a week after the attack, I was at my cousin Cathy's house in Massachusetts. When she heard I was going to a wedding with a black eye, she had called my mother immediately.

"Bring Chrissy over," she'd said. "I'll fix her up. Nobody will ever know."

As I sat in a kid's chair, low to the ground, Cathy patted under my eye with some kind of cream and my aunt told her to give my cheeks some color as well.

"It looks much better," Cathy said after it was over.

I had returned home for the wedding of a friend I had known for thirty-five years. I would see people I hadn't seen since I was seventeen. I had warned my friends Susan, Molly, and Carrie about my black eye.

"Sweetie," they said. "It looks better than we thought it would. You look beautiful. That must have been awful."

They held my hand. They hugged my mother. Friends from every period of my childhood were there. My now-retired high school librarian and I talked about politics, and his presence at the wedding was comforting. Like me, he couldn't wait for the White House to change hands.

"Hillary, Obama, Edwards . . . I don't care who it is, just let it be somebody."

The last time I had seen the school's librarian, I was a shy little girl who only said "nice" things. Now I was a forty-year-old woman with a black eye who had defended a dissertation on Italian literature and two small children from a man with a hard fist. During the entirety of the reception, I barely stood. I sat in a chair as longtime friends moved in and out of my circle in a steady embrace.

On the last day of my trip, I visited my grandmother. It would be my last visit with her. Grandma didn't recognize me when I arrived, but after my mother explained a number of times who I was, it suddenly clicked.

"Oh," she said with a giddy excitement I hadn't seen in her in years. "Oh, oh, oh . . ."

We held hands, each with tears in our eyes, and although she didn't say anything more, I treasured the connection we made that day. I was not surprised in the midst of her dementia, Grandma, the woman who had drawn me out of my shell as a child, would be the person who connected me to the world again.

Retrogression 6:
September 15, 2007, 10:55 p.m.

We arrive home. My children and I sit in the car as my husband walks through every room in our house, every room, searching for bad guys everywhere.

Chapter 6:
Little Man

I began to watch my son sleep a few nights after my children and I were attacked. Something about the rise and fall of his chest quieted me. One night, from this peacefulness came my unexpected sobs. Samuel opened his eyes and stared at me, surprised. He sat, kissed me on my cheek, and just as suddenly lay back down and fell into a deep sleep.

I never knew how Samuel would react to the attack, so I sat in anxious vigil. Most of the time, while I waited nervously for proof my son had been permanently damaged, Samuel went on asking the same three-year-old questions he had always asked.

"Why is the sky blue?"

"Why do cars drive?"

"Do dogs dream?"

"God—does he live in Madagascar?"

"Why do we call on phones?"

I was relieved every time a new colorful question came out, and often laughed out loud, but I still found myself standing over his bed at night, watching him sleep.

We were at an October birthday party and kids were running in circles in the park, back and forth from the playground to the picnic benches. Three dads played horseshoes, and as one man swung his horseshoe back, he gouged open the smooth forehead of his son, who had crept up behind him to watch. I didn't see it. I was talking with a friend when the dad ran over holding his child. Blood poured from the child's face, dyeing his and his father's shirts red.

I had always been able to handle blood. In fact, it was my husband who paced nervously and stayed home to look after whoever wasn't bleeding while I calmly took the injured one to the emergency room. But this time I burst into tears, grabbed the hand of my son, and escaped before anyone could see me cry.

My son and I walked through the park along a series of small pathways, farther and farther away from the gathering. He remained quiet and at times would stroke my hand, much like he had rubbed my face the day of the attack.

"That bad guy won't hurt you again, Mom. I think they caught him and put him in jail."

That the little boy's blood had reminded him, too, of our attack brought on fresh tears. Finally, I crouched and slid my arm around his back.

"My sweet little man. I'm sure he's in jail."

We went to a family therapist.

"The kids are okay. They're upset but not doing anything out of the ordinary given the trauma you experienced together."

I resisted. "Sam's not the same. He's hitting kids on the playground. He doesn't listen to me. He thinks I'm weak. He told me so."

"He's getting cues from you. He believes you aren't strong because you don't feel strong. Once you have healed, this will go away. You'll see."

"But he hides from black men," I said. "I'm not sure what to do?"

"Tell him what you're thinking. Just be honest," the therapist said.

One morning, as I dropped Samuel off at school, he turned to me and whispered, "I don't like Roland because he wears a black shirt. It makes me nervous."

I pulled him into a quiet area of the classroom. "Honey, if somebody is good to you or kind, that's all that matters. If somebody doesn't treat you right, then it's okay to say he or she has hurt you. But don't say you don't like someone because of a shirt. That's not fair."

I paused to let it sink in.

"What if somebody said they didn't like you because you were wearing your walrus shirt?"

"Pooh doesn't like my walrus shirt. He's afraid of walruses."

"I know, and you don't like that, do you?"

"No, it makes me sad when Pooh won't play with me."

Pooh, a boy at daycare nicknamed after the beloved Winnie the Pooh, was terrified of walruses and ran from Samuel each time he wore his shirt. Sam continued to talk about Pooh, hurt and somewhat defiant, and I could see he understood.

As I held hands with my son in the park, for the first time that week I sensed the blue sky still held promises for us, even in this newly discovered world where politically correct language didn't solve real problems. Soon my son found a rock and stopped to draw with it in the sand. Then we spoke about pirates.

"Ahoy there, matey!" he said as we walked by some people.

"Ahoy," they all said.

Then a bridge that crossed over a river became a boat and it carried us to the playground where the kids from the party ate popsicles. A little boy wore a large Band-Aid on his forehead with a scene from Snow White on it. No ambulance had come to take him away. No father sat next to his son by a hospital bed regretting a good day gone horribly wrong. It had all been okay.

"Ahoy there," Sam said, looking at the boy with the Band-Aid.

"Ahoy there," he replied, and I realized I was breathing again.

Retrogression 7:
September 15, 2007, 10:54 p.m.

We turn onto my street. My neighbors are all in their houses, soft lights poking through their blinds. Mark pulls into the center of our driveway. "You left no room for my . . ." I begin to say. But my car is locked shut in a parking lot, the keys in someone else's hand.

Chapter 7: Dreamy Girl

Ada is a dreamy girl. She's similar to me, especially when I was her age—completely in her own world, trusting, sweet. She often looks out into the distance with a smile on her face and I know something's going on inside, but I'm never sure what. An event or thought finds itself on a page of her notebook hours later in poetic, drawing or story form: two girls sit next to each other on a bench in elegant dresses that bunch to the side; a mom pushes a shopping cart and her blue-eyed daughter skips next to her in a fanciful, colorful dress; a boy steps on a bumblebee and cries; a woman, covered in blood, lies on a cot in an ambulance.

When she was two, Ada attended preschool three days a week. She didn't say a word the entire year until the last day of school. But she knew how to swing for hours on the playground and she could draw her heart out, Dante's *visibile parlare*. We love Ada's dreaminess, her broad strokes of the pen, her faraway gaze. The fairies she creates with their magic dust are just what we need most of the time.

Sam has a dreaminess, too, but it's tied to a practical quality. "Sometimes I wish I were smaller so I could sit on the car wheel and ride it like a Ferris Wheel," he once told me. "You could take me to school that way." Sam's practicality grounds him and his tree-trunk strength and stubbornness mean he can accomplish anything he sets his mind to. He dreams big, but he also knows how to avoid the pitfalls. Ada retreats into her drawings and only through them do we know she is suffering. The night in the parking lot plays out in the background of almost every drawing now.

Shortly after the attack, I overhear my children talking about Polly Pocket, a doll that fits into even the smallest of pockets. Ada is showing Polly to Sam, holding the tiny doll in her hands.

"And you named her Polly Pocket?" Sam asks.

"No, the world named her Polly Pocket," Ada responds in a dreamy voice.

Retrogression 8:
September 15, 2007, 10:40 p.m.

The sound of the car engine is melodic. I can't hold on to my thoughts long enough to resolve them—the grant application that's due next week, Ada's and Sam's dental appointments, my body's achiness, exams that need grading. I wonder if I should tell my mother about what just happened. I turn and look at my kids. They are so quiet. And Mark, he keeps taking his hand off the steering wheel and touching my shoulder.

Chapter 8: Fatherhood

"**W**hat's happening to black men in this country?" Mark said one evening when I arrived home from work. His New Zealand accent seemed particularly strong, as it often does when he is agitated about something.

"What do you mean?" I asked.

He pulled up a news story online. A University of North Carolina student, president of her class, had been shot to death by two black men after they had abducted her from her home and driven to as many ATMs as they could with her cards.

After reading the article and acknowledging out loud what my husband hadn't mentioned, that this could have been me or the kids a few months earlier, I commented, "Look, just as many murders are committed in this country by white men."

"True," my husband said. "But if you look at the population, the proportion of white men in this country and the proportion of black men, it's very different. A much larger percentage of black men are committing murders."

We looked online for some figures. Approximately the same number of white and black men committed murder in the United States in the year 2000. What didn't match up, however, was the percentage of white people in relation to black in this country: 75 percent to 12.3 percent.

"When is this country really going to talk about race? You are participating in two discussion groups on this topic, but do you ever talk about these things? Every day I go to school and most of my white students have a contact number for their fathers and most of my black students don't. Where the hell are they? And if I said this to anybody but you, I'd be called a racist."

We went on to talk about how most black men who do commit murders kill somebody who is also black (90 percent), but the most talked about crimes, the ones that make it to the news, are when black men kill white women or men. Nicole Simpson's blond, blond hair contrasted with the dark skin of O.J. Simpson took up two years of front-page news.

"And the North Carolina student . . . Are the lives of black women and men any less important?" I asked.

"I see what you mean," my husband said. "But that doesn't change my point. There is a problem here in the United States, and it involves the fact that black men aren't raising their children and young black men often don't have role models. But nobody will talk about this side of things. I agree it's unfair but how can anything change if we are only talking about half the problem?"

I couldn't disagree with my husband, yet I felt uncomfortable agreeing. I was more at ease talking about black disadvantage, how slaves must have passed on an intolerably low sense of self-worth to their children, which continued to affect black people for generations. How black men were made to feel about themselves and all that followed must be taken into consideration during discussions on race. And although

Mark was comfortable with the language, often agreed and understood the landscape, he could no longer passionately defend it.

My husband had been thinking about fathers long before the kids and I were attacked. He was born in Los Angeles. His New Zealander mother had fallen in love with and married a California pharmacist, then moved to the States. When Mark was three months old, his mother moved back to New Zealand and left her husband because he had become addicted to amphetamines. Mark loves to tell how at the airport a sympathetic Marlon Brando purchased a stuffed animal for Mark's older brother, who wouldn't stop crying.

In America, Mark's father tried to remarry without ever having divorced, while in New Zealand, Mark and his brother lived in a foster home for three years. When he was four, Mark remembers looking through the car's back window, tears rolling down his face, as his foster family receded from view and a new life with his mom, brother, and mother's new husband began.

At four and a half, news came that Mark's father had died from a drug overdose. It was this idea of his father—addicted, absent, and dead—that influenced how he perceived fathers throughout his lifetime, and it was no surprise that in graduate school he wrote a three-hundred-page dissertation on the father figure in nineteenth-century American literature before he settled into his occupation as a high school English teacher.

When I met Mark, I was living in Seattle. It was a slow seduction neither of us recognized. We were both involved in other imperfect relationships and would often talk about the dreariness of it all over a bottle of wine. The day we went to an Al Gore speech in '91—full of hope that the young presidential front-runners, Clinton and Gore, could change the world and make the nation feel young again—was the first time I understood something could happen between us. Mark towers above me and so I gave him my hand and let him steer me through the crowd of students and faculty, almost to the front.

It was not his New Zealand accent I admired when I first met Mark. I was attracted to his nonmainstream views of America, his cynicism about the world coupled with an optimism about what it could become.

My husband is balding, but when I first met him, he had lots of fine, blond hair, the kind of hair nobody in my family ever has. He is tall with blue eyes. He often frowns when he is thinking. When we started dating, I would push his patience, at times to the point where most people might have exploded. But Mark always came back with a cool, rational answer that considered my perspective. If he reconsidered his ideas, he told me why. If he still disagreed with me, he explained why, too. I often asked his opinion when it came to politics, religion, and many other topics.

Mark and I left our jobs and lives in Seattle in '95 to attend graduate school in North Carolina. During our graduate school years, we participated in open debates with our peers about presidential scandals, women's rights, racism, literature, and freedom of speech. My husband's views always sat to the far left.

After graduate school, Mark began teaching sophomores and juniors at a public high school in Atlanta, Georgia. Early on he remarked, after collecting student information cards, that most black students in the class didn't list contact information for their fathers. He had viewed this as a commentary on society's horrible treatment of black men in the past, which had led to a terrible struggle, awful feelings of inadequacy, and low self-worth.

Then I was attacked.

"Do you know how much I love my students?" my husband said. "Do you know how much I want more for them? I am ready to find their fathers, grab them by the scruff of their necks, and tell them how they're sticking it to their kids. I'm their children's teacher. I see their sons for an hour and a half five times a week, but some students see more of me than they do their own fathers. Many of them give up. They don't try. They say they're victims, that they don't have a chance. But if I let them use that as an excuse, then I'm agreeing with them, confirming they don't. And they do. They all do. No excuses."

"And what about you? Did you have a chance when your father left you?" I asked.

"Yes, of course I did," he said.

Retrogression 9:

September 15, 2007, 10:30 p.m.

Beth Orton's "Pass in Time" quietly states, "So much stays unknown till the time you are strong." My children are in the backseat of the car, far away. I pull down the visor and look at my eye in the mirror. Orton sings, "This time is whatever I want it to mean" and nobody else says a word.

Chapter 9:
Fatherhood, Take Two

Shortly after the teacher's strike that had landed him in jail when I was ten, my father sat us down and told us that under no circumstances were we ever to say the N-word. He described what black men and women had experienced and why the word was offensive. I don't recall a specific event that provoked this family meeting, but I assume he had been reminded of how much he hated the word after hearing it used while he was in jail.

More than thirty years later, I was charged with talking about the book *Nigger* by Randall Kennedy. The Transform Project group I led was small. In addition to four college students, our group was composed of a thirty-seven-year-old woman who worked at a hospital, my student leader, and me.

We began by discussing how we would address the word itself in our conversation. Adrianne, a black freshman, said she had heard the word so often she felt the need to tackle it right on—use it without shame. Thirty-seven-year-old Ruth, a white woman, said she would say it, but she would understand if others didn't. My coleader agreed with Adrianne. As a black student, James had heard the N-word too often not to say it. Ellen, a student from Japan, and Lester, a white male student, said they were okay either way. I was the only person who would have trouble saying this word. As a result of my discomfort, nobody said it for the remainder of the conversation.

I decided to facilitate discussions for my university's Transform Project shortly after I was attacked. Not only was I tired of answering questions about the race of my attacker, but the idea of learning something from this experience became the driving force behind my existence; if I could learn, it might not all be for nothing.

African Americans had worked at my university since its inception, first as slaves and then as wage laborers. Although the university had been a leader in the desegregation of higher education in the South, it also had a very troubling racial past and things had come to a head during the 2003–04 academic year, when a white professor had said "a nigger in the woodpile" at a departmental faculty gathering. The fallout was explosive, further complicated when two international students showed up at a university-hosted Halloween party in blackface. The Transform Project was developed in response to the escalated tensions from these two events, which proved to be just the tip of the iceberg.

My history with the Transform Project went back to the summer before my attack. Fortunately, when I was attacked, a support network was already in place as a result of our lunch discussions on race. When I confessed to the group I had told my children the man was probably poor and stole my purse because he needed money, a black woman said my children could extend this description to all black people. "I have a job," she said. "I don't steal."

I told my current group that when I first read Kennedy's book, I began to cry when I realized the child's poem "Eeny Meeny Miny Moe" originally used the line "Catch a nigger [not tiger] by the toe." How many times had I used that rhyme to settle a dispute on the playground without ever knowing its origins? How many other offensive things had I said in ignorance during my lifetime? I probably didn't want to know.

As our discussion continued, I began to feel old. Having recently turned forty, I realized I was a generation ahead of most people in the room. James and I asked our group what the N word meant to each of us. When it came to me, I responded that during my childhood the N-word was absolutely off-limits. The success of the strike my father took part in—the school instituted a maternity leave policy for teachers, allowing many women to keep their jobs after having babies—had spilled over into other justice issues. When my father saw how easy it was to talk about his beliefs with his children, how we had rallied around his decision to break the law and strike because, as he had put it, "laws were made by people and sometimes people make mistakes," he began to tell us about other wrongs.

I explained to the group that even when I went to college and ate lunch at a table where most of our school's black students sat every day, I did not hear this word tossed around. Perhaps, I said, it was because I was there that the black students didn't use the N-word, but I also assumed it was still taboo in 1985.

My students explained that as rap music became more popular, so did the N-word. The black students in my group said they heard the N-word daily. Adrianne was sick of the N-word. James spoke of the idea of reclaiming the word, redefining it, and using it in a better way. As a child, Lester had called his father the N-word casually one day, not knowing what it meant, after hearing it at school. He remembered his father's face, the punishment that followed, the sting of his father's words. Yet overwhelmingly, the sentiment of my students reflected James's desire to take back the word, a process that had already begun through the efforts of his generation.

Our conversation flowed easily, and I forgot the tension that seemed to arrive every time I led my group through this murky territory. In the past I had always asked myself if I had been too blunt or insensitive. Did I say the right thing? Respond in the right way? Could I have offended or slighted anyone? This day I didn't worry. We were all hearing each other, connecting. So much so that before I realized, I was recounting a conversation my husband and I recently had about his students, most of them black, fatherless men. Was there a correlation between these statistics and crime? I found myself asking my group. Just the other day, my husband had wondered if there was. The room became silent.

I waited for the silence to diminish and when it didn't, I said, "I don't know what to say to my husband. I'm sure there are blind spots, but I don't even know them. I'm blind, too. I suggested my husband go and talk to his principal. He's African American and perhaps he could get my husband to see things in a different way. But he didn't think it was a good idea—it would be embarrassing, racist even, to single out this one guy and assume he could be some kind of spokesman for his race."

Nobody looked up. The ease of the conversation just a few minutes before had been replaced with a dull ache. I suddenly felt younger than my students. What was I, a white, Italian American woman, doing leading a discussion on race? Why did I ever think I could do this?

We had a half an hour left when Lester looked at me and said, "What would the administrator say to your husband? He could go into his office and say, 'Look, most of my black students don't have fathers.' And the administrator would look at his figures and say, 'Yes. You're right.' And then what? What would he accomplish? Perhaps your husband needs to do more research. Perhaps all of the white families come from one part of town, the part with two-parent households, and the black students are from a poorer area, where, if there were white students, they would be from broken homes too."

True, most of the black students took the bus from a poorer area of town. Still, I didn't feel comfortable equating poverty with single-parenthood. I thought of my husband's comments about making his principal a representative of his race. There was always a good reason for not talking.

I, too, resented being a representative of the short woman's club. Friends constantly said to me, "You'll like her. She's short like you, has a lot of spunk, and she's loud!" But usually this preface soured me to the meeting.

And I had done the same thing to a gay friend one time. "You'll love Don and Ray. They're a great couple."

"Do you think I'll like them because they're gay?" my friend had asked me.

Yet once, at a workshop, three short women and I were put together in a group and asked to make a list. What did we want others to understand about short people? What did we want them to stop doing?

"Stop pairing us up with other short people," we wrote.

"Don't assume we aren't intelligent or experienced just because we look young."

"Don't talk down to us."

"Don't assume we can't lift or do things."

"Don't ignore us in line or call on tall people first."

Our list went on and on and it was the longest list at the workshop. It had been the first time anybody had ever asked us this question.

Christine Ristaino 39

I thought back to the workshop, to the high I had felt afterward, and I wondered if this tiptoeing, this tiresome dance, our refusal to lay these topics out there all thorny . . . I wondered if all this were faulty.

Retrogression 10:
September 15, 2007, 10:25 p.m.

We drive home in my husband's car, windows open. I can see the top of shop signs disappearing from the side view mirror then bright lights interspersed with the darkness of trees.

Chapter 10: Search Terms

"Attack" and "Support Group" and "Atlanta." "Attacked" and "Support Group" and "Atlanta." "Attack" and "Support Group." "Mugged" and "Support Group" and "Atlanta." "Assault" and "Resources" and "Atlanta." "Assault" and "Resources." "Assaulted" and "Resources." "Assaulted" and "Support Group." "Hit by a stranger" and "Support Group" and "Atlanta." "Hit and beaten in front of children by a stranger who had been sitting on a bench in a parking lot" and "Support Group" and "Atlanta."

After we were attacked, I plugged in search terms online, looking for help. The overwhelming number of resources were for victims of rape, domestic violence, and sexual abuse. I googled for hours but couldn't find anything for plain old violent assaults. So I toyed with the idea of attending a rape survivors' meeting. I would go and tell my story.

"Well, a man hit me a number of times in the face, messed up my nose, stole my purse, left me on the ground bleeding. Oh, and he scared my children."

Perhaps there would be silence.

"And then what happened?" somebody would say.

"Nothing."

For a while I thought a domestic abuse group might have the resources we needed.

"So how many nights in a row did this happen?"

"Once."

"Are you afraid he'll do it again?"

"Well, no."

"Are you and your children in danger?"

"Um, no."

"Do you need the name of a shelter?"

I gave up. The terms available in our culture just didn't exist for my search. There was nothing for us—no group where I could go and talk; no place where I could hear the stories of others. I did, however, find an article in an online newspaper by an elderly woman who had been mugged years before. She told how in her community she had worn the label of "the woman who had been mugged" for forty years, and how after her experience she had never been the same.

In the absence of a group, I joined a social justice class on diversity. Since the main goal of the class was to explore race and ethnicity, and my attack had created so much confusion in me about this topic, I decided to sign up.

Often we were assigned group work during class and the groups we formed were always multicultural. However, two months into the curriculum we were asked to separate along racial lines in the hope we would communicate in a more personal way with people who had experienced race in a similar manner. White people were to meet with other white people.

African Americans would meet with African Americans. The one twist involved a statement after the instructions saying we really should put ourselves into the group we identified with the most. It didn't have to be the one in which society would place us, and we could create our own group if necessary.

The two African Americans, a graying man in his sixties and a tall woman in her forties, moved to a corner of the room. They sat facing each other in two soft chairs and I immediately wanted to join them in this intimate setting. Sixteen white people moved to the center of the room. They spanned from their early twenties to mid-sixties; had red, white, gray, brown, and blond hair and sets of blue, brown, or green eyes; and were a variety of heights, ranging from just a bit taller than me to up to six foot four or five inches. They moved around noisily and comfortably, laughing and conversing as they picked up their papers, pens, notebooks, cups, and paper plates, bustling toward the center of the room. I was about to join them when Eloise, one of the class leaders, decided she was going to form her own group based on ethnic rather than racial identity. I knew I would feel comfortable in this group.

The ethnic group was composed of four women. One, a woman in her early fifties, had a strong Jewish upbringing and identified herself more on ethnic than racial lines. Another, Eloise, had been raised by Jewish parents who, while trying to become part of white, northern culture, had decided to downplay their ethnicity. Although her parents rejected their identity, her classmates provided daily, painful reminders of her differences. As an adult, Eloise clung to her Judaism in reaction to her parents' rejection of it. The third woman had studied Judaism in college and identified more with the women in the stories she had read than with her own white Protestant family. I was the only Italian American in the group, but when the people in my group spoke of being an outsider and not quite understanding why, I felt as though they were talking about me. For lack of anything else, we called ourselves the "not quite fitting into the dominant white culture" group. When the class reconvened, one representative from each section was charged with reading the group notes out loud. I volunteered and began reporting our findings.

As I read, the room became silent. Many of the people listening stared with arms folded in front of them. I spoke about the term we had come up with to define ourselves, and one or two people chuckled. When I relayed details about the group feeling slightly outside the margins as a result of our ethnicity, economic situation, or looks, only one person nodded. As we were leaving, I walked to the other coleader of the program, Renee, to give her what had become our traditional end-of-the-evening hug. Renee, a New Yorker in her early sixties, had spent the majority of her adult life in the South in the lesbian minority. Renee saw me and backed away.

"I am just so angry," she said. "What's wrong with being white? What, you are better than us? You want to disclaim the white privilege you grew up with? And what is it with this name you have given yourselves, 'don't associate with white privilege' or something like that? Is that a get-out-of-jail-free card—if you decide you're not part of the white group, then suddenly you don't have to take responsibility for white privilege?"

I'll admit, I had struggled with the idea of white privilege. I had grown up with four siblings living on a teacher's salary and none of us had felt monetarily privileged. However, through this course I realized I indeed benefited from white privilege on a daily basis. And lately I felt respected, at home and in my career. Renee's comments were jarring and unsettling.

That evening the class received an email from a different member of the white group, a woman who had lived in the South her entire life and was in her mid-sixties. She remembered our title as "those who didn't identify with the privilege of the dominant group" and wrote that white people can be critical of white privilege and not want to be identified with it, but have to admit they have it. She ended with the following statement: "So it just didn't seem fair. It felt as though the people in the 'other' group had found a way to be not quite as 'white' as the 'white' group. A way to 'trump' us."

I responded, writing that our title didn't have the word privilege in it. It was not that we didn't feel we had privilege, but during our childhoods, we all in some way had felt a bit marginalized by white culture even though, ironically, we are all white.

Emails flew. Some supported my position and some didn't.

The final message, written by a woman who was in her sixties as well, said, "I felt similarly to some of you, in that I thought 'How convenient to not have to feel responsible for all evils done by the white race.' I would very much like to be able to step out of the 'WHITE' race and I as well feel discriminated against by the larger society because of my sexual preference and gender. I have been disappointed at times that these minorities have not been recognized in this curriculum."

On the surface, it seemed as though I hadn't been heard at all, but a line in the last message changed how I viewed the conflict, for it touched on something I hadn't considered. I thought back to the instructions for this activity. We were asked to separate into groups based on race. Creating an ethnic group was somewhat beyond the search terms. Sexual preference would have been an even greater leap. My group had found a loophole, but it was not large enough to house all the people who had been marginalized by white culture. Members of the ethnic group had done what the lesbian members of our class had only wished they could do.

At our next meeting a few weeks later, I walked into the building and sat on one of the congregation's foldout metal chairs. I remembered this feeling from long-over childhood days and tried to maneuver my new role in the group—suddenly a bit on the periphery, a location where I had this time willingly put myself. It occurred to me I felt more at home here in the margins, so I sat up straight and waited for more conversations to experience what the search would reveal.

Retrogression 11:
September 15, 2007,
10:18 p.m. and 2 seconds.

Once seat-belted in, I put my hands over my cheeks, feel my wrists touch and support each other. I cradle the bottom of my face with my hands and draw strength from them.

Chapter 11: Messiah Complex

She has taken it upon herself to be the "messiah" of figuring out these racial differences and barriers. . . .

—A high school student's comments after reading sections of *All the Silent Spaces*

As my book develops, I begin to wonder if my stories can help high school students cope with and talk about difficult subjects, especially their struggles with race and violence. As a teenager, I never had the tools to do this. I email the Freedom Writers Association, a nonprofit group dedicated to empowering students of all identities and economic situations in the classroom, and ask if teachers would include some of my stories in their curriculum. I'm hoping to gain knowledge from students of a variety of backgrounds, especially those who have experienced race differently than I have. The Freedom Writers Association is a good place to help me connect with these students, since it works with urban schools from all over the country.

I send my first and last chapters, which are letters written to my attacker, as well as a few accounts of the discussions I have had on race, to Maria, a Freedom Writers teacher who works in a large urban school district in Chicago. A month later Maria sends me an envelope filled with her high school student responses. I pore over them. Student reactions to my writings are mixed, some very upbeat, others quite unenthusiastic. I cover my floor with essays, choose quotes from the pages that affect me most, and pin them onto the bulletin board in my office. Each day I read a different quote out loud and try to glean something from it.

On Monday I read the first student's words: "If I was a child and my mom was attacked, I would have nightmares at night just like the kids."

Tuesday's quote comforts me by saying, "This is no one's fault. Do not feel sad, or regret anything, let your daughter know why you didn't hug her . . . I am proud that you are trying to help people."

On Wednesday, a student says although she doesn't understand the purpose of my book, she enjoyed reading my work just the same. She follows this statement with, "I think."

Thursday's student gives me insight into my son: "Her son seems to have been greatly affected by this. He has turned to violence himself to be able to protect himself and his mom when he grows up."

On Friday, a student tells me that writing these pages and focusing so much on the attack is unhealthy. She says I need to move on. I wonder if she's right.

The following week I pick up where I left off. Monday's student stands up for me and reading her words reassures me: "She said people were talking about what they would do. People shouldn't speak like that, most people freeze up in panic, they don't know what they would have done."

Another student's words, "She is brave," bring a warmth to my chest and keep me going on Tuesday.

Wednesday, a girl who has spent a lot of time on the streets describes people she knows who commit petty and violent crimes. She doubts they feel any remorse.

On Thursday, a boy talks about his family's experience with violence. "My own mother was even mugged by a black man, and although this didn't have a lasting impact on me—it very well may have left one on my mom."

A male student's comments on Friday are sobering: "Race matters in this world. . . . It took a brutal beat-down from a black man to realize what she truly needed to do. . . . She realized that racism runs deep. I should know this, too, for I have been looked upon by people; people who fear 'my kind.'"

I save the comments that challenge me the most for the third week. The four quotes I read from Monday to Thursday ultimately change my book.

On Monday, a student says I am making too big a deal of this. She admits everyone needs a healing period but says, "I don't think it is necessary to try to make the world believe you are out to change the world!"

When I read Tuesday's quote, I laugh, but the writer makes an impression on me. "Chapter one to the Letter to the man we met on September 15, 2007 is very pointless! There was no reason for her to even write it! . . . And I want to stop reading when she wrote 'Perhaps I understand now why the abused wife returns to her husband!' Come on, the lady got jumped! Nowhere near getting abused by your husband everyone!" I love her spirit but a nauseous feeling in my stomach reminds me that she doesn't know everything. It hits me that even close friends and family don't know about my history with violence.

A student's comments on Wednesday make me realize for sure I have to change the beginning and ending to my book. She doesn't like the letter format I use and challenges me to rewrite these pieces because, in her opinion, they read like a sentimental novel with the perfect happy ending. She gives me advice about the prologue: "At the very least, she could have started off the chapter with a brief overview of what happened to her and how the public and media reacted to it." I know she's right, but I want the happy ending so much. I need it! Because of this student's advice, I take the two letters out of my book altogether.

The insights I read on Thursday hit me hard. I take it as a sign there's some truth to them: "The woman who writes about her encounter with a criminal talks as though people don't get mugged every day. I feel like she thinks she is alone in the situation, and the only person who has been affected by robbery. She has taken it upon herself to be the 'messiah' of figuring out these racial differences and barriers. . . . The reality is that in the city, people get mugged and worse—killed, regardless of their race. . . . I am sure this woman's attacker is not looking for forgiveness, I'm sure the incident does not faze him. Those who steal only think about themselves. They are not eager to sit down and have a nice long chat."

I stay with these four quotes, read them over and over again. Then I see my first and last chapters for what they really are—a way to process what happened, a way to tell off my attacker, and a way to begin.

I decide, if I am really going to do this, I have to be more honest with myself about what's driving me. The man who molested me and my rapist—I find their faces in my memory, look at them, really look, and begin to uncover my story with them. I go back into my writings, into all the silent spaces, and add them into my story.

That night I ask my husband to read the latest version of my memoir. "You're still doing exactly what this student says you're doing—you're trying to find meaning here. Do you always have to find meaning? Can't you have experiences that mean nothing?" I relay this conversation to my friend, Felix, over coffee. I play with my spoon, laughing and looking down after one of Felix's bad jokes. "Jesus as a stand-up comic," he says. "Take my life, please . . ."

Retrogression 12:
September 15, 2007, 10:17 p.m.

I open the door to my husband's car on the passenger side and slide onto the warm seat. I pull the seat belt down and snap it into place.

Chapter 12: Wolves

I've told my children to eat, brush their teeth, comb their hair, and put on their shoes at least ten times. Finally, I carry them out and place them into their car seats, shoeless—each holding a piece of toast. "Neither of you is listening to a word I say," I tell them. When I drop my children off at school, they both smile at me and wave, and my anger dissolves.

In the afternoon, I pick them up and we drive home. We have half an hour to get Ada ready for her aikido lesson, a class on self-defense I insisted she take after the attack. I pull out her *gi* and place it on the chair next to her, nodding for her to put it on. After twenty minutes, Ada is still sitting on the floor in her underwear, staring at the white uniform.

"Ada," I say, "please put on your *gi*. We're going to be late."

"I am," she tells me, but when I look at her three minutes later, Ada hasn't moved.

I grab the pants and put them on her. I place the aikido top over each shoulder. When the top is on, I tie the two ties, grab Ada's shoes in one hand and my daughter in the other, carry her to the car, open the door, plop her in her seat, and return to pick up Samuel.

"Come on, Sam," I say. "We're late." I carry him to the car and place him in his booster.

Now where's Ada? I look around. She's picking flowers. "Come on, Ada," I yell. I strap her into the car. We're off.

When we arrive home after aikido, my husband is outside talking with our neighbor, who has locked himself out of his house. He's going to try a few things, but if he can't get in, Mark and I decide we'll invite him over for dinner. The living room and kitchen are a mess, toys everywhere, crayons all over the table, toilet paper wrapped around every piece of furniture by Sam.

"Ada, Sam," I say, "please can you help Mom and Dad clean the living room?"

Neither child moves.

"Come on," I say. "We need your help."

"I'm not helping," Ada announces.

"Ada, Mom and Dad help you all the time. We're not asking for much. Most of this is your and Sam's mess."

"It's not," Ada says.

"Yes, it is," I say.

I begin to rail about my children to my husband in front of them. "They have been like this all day. I don't know what to do with them."

"Kids, if you're not going to help us, then you need to go upstairs to your rooms," Mark says.

Both children march upstairs.

Five minutes later Samuel returns. "Mom, I'll help," he says. "Ada won't because she's running away."

"She is?"

"Yes. What should we do?"

"I don't know, Sam. Hopefully she won't run away. I'll really miss her," I say.

I go outside to invite my neighbor over for dinner. As I'm talking with him, I watch my daughter slip barefoot past me and begin to walk down the street.

"Ada," I say. "Are you going to run away?"

"I'm running away now," she responds.

I walk behind her and we almost make it to the end of the street. It's hot and humid outside, we're both sweating, and Ada steps on a small piece of glass. She lifts her foot gingerly and looks at me, her mouth open and eyes wide. I carry her back. We use tweezers to pull out the glass and Ada screams the whole time. We eat dinner late, seven thirty, without my neighbor, who is by now safely inside his own home. Then it's time for bed. Mark leads the children upstairs and I begin to clear the table, but when I look up, Ada is standing in front of me, tears sliding down her face.

"I had a terrible day," she says.

"I know," I say. "We both did, didn't we?"

"I can't stop feeling sad," Ada says.

"I'm sorry," I say and I take her into my arms. I sit on the couch and rock her. "I'm the luckiest mom," I tell her. She continues to cry.

"Mom, I feel like the little girl in room 205."

Room 205. I know the number is significant, but I can't remember where I've heard it before. Then I remember. It's a book Ada took out of the library that talks about a girl whose relative had put his hands in her pants.

I steer Ada's face toward mine and look into her eyes. I can barely breathe. Finally, I am able to get the words out. "Tell me why you feel like that little girl," I whisper.

"Because it says she feels alone and quiet," she says.

"Did anyone touch you like they touched that girl?" I ask.

"No, Mommy. But I keep thinking, what if I ran away and you didn't chase me? It's dark now and I would be all alone and then I would worry about the wolves hurting me. When I think of that, I feel like the girl in the book."

"It's okay, darling. You're here with me. I did see you. You're home now."

"But what if you didn't see me?"

"But I did," I say.

Retrogression 13:

September 15, 2007, 10:15 p.m.

Children wind around my legs, nourished by neon liquid sugar. My husband calls to them and takes their hands. My children jump from foot to foot. They talk, drink, dribble, spill their blood-red juice onto my husband's tired feet.

Chapter 13: Grandma, Wendy, and ~~Anne~~

I love the way I feel after my students take a test. Following a week of review and questions, nobody knocks on my door and it's calm. This is what it's been like lately—as though the test is over and I can relax.

My grandmother died at ninety-six. The day it happened, a nurse called my mother, who arrived quickly and, eyes locked with my grandmother's, talked her into the afterlife. After an hour, my grandmother closed her eyes for the last time and my mother sobbed into the arms of the Jamaican nurse who had been caring for my grandmother for four years.

My mother asks me to write the eulogy for my grandmother, and so I begin writing about a woman whose decisions were at times controversial. She was the wife of an alcoholic and had to work full time at a diner to support her family. She made broomstick skirts for her daughters and beautiful hats. She would periodically pack up the rat-infested apartment where her family lived and move while my grandfather was at the bar, only to find him at her doorstep a few weeks later, begging to be taken back. When my grandmother moved her three daughters to Texas years later, she finally made a permanent break from my grandfather and then took on a series of men friends well into her eighties. At her daughters' request, I don't talk about this part of my grandmother's life in her eulogy. Instead I focus on how she had stepped in as a mother figure when her own daughter, my mother, was ill.

As a teen, I was awkward and shy. It was not that I didn't know how to talk to others, but more that I didn't even realize I should talk to them. Throughout my childhood, I was more likely to observe rather than participate. I often sat on my grandmother's lap at the table and soaked in the conversations around me.

One Christmas, my cousin took me to a party at her friend's house. The room was filled with high school juniors who were two years older than me. Because I didn't know them, I sat and listened as everyone talked, and conversations circled around me. At one point the room became silent while a girl spoke about violence she had experienced in a van. She laughed uncomfortably as she talked about it, and everyone remained quiet, as intent on listening as I had been the whole night. Her words floated by me, making very little sense until Wendy explained to me later that the girl had been raped. Wendy told my aunt I hadn't spoken at the party, and this information trickled over to my mother, who awkwardly and sweetly tried to cultivate my social skills.

At fourteen, the year of Wendy's party, I was completely lost in the day-to-day activities of bringing up children. I had become proficient at this job at age eight and raising children was something I did well. In third grade, in a picture book about myself, I wrote that my favorite food was spaghetti and my favorite thing to do involved "touching Milo," an innocent reference to a motherly instinct that had kicked in early, in second grade, the day my mother brought Milo home from the hospital and I began rocking him in the old rocking chair. By the time Zach arrived, I was almost fourteen and my mother fell silently into a depression that would last a number of years.

When my parents married, my mother quit her job to be a stay-at-home mom, a decision they felt strongly would be worth any material sacrifices they would have to make along the way. Fortunately for us, even on those days when we seemed to have little in our refrigerator, our parents found a way to pull together delicious home-cooked meals. My mother's creative sewing skills provided us with clothes to brave all four seasons. Although at times we complained we didn't have what we wanted, we always had what we needed. More importantly, we knew we were loved.

By the time I was fourteen, there were five children in our house. My grandmother often appeared at just the right time. She placed cookies on the table, and as soon as she had removed the plastic wrap from the dish, my brothers and I devoured them. During these visits, grandma talked quietly. "We have to do something. She doesn't talk. We never know what she's thinking. She's so shy."

When a black girl named Anne started tormenting me at swim classes, my grandmother began to show up to lessons. During class, my grandmother witnessed Anne yank a ribbon that held my hair back and throw it in the pool for "no apparent reason."

"She hates me, Grandma," I said.

Anne was an only child and I often thought she might be lonely. During class, she usually offered to help me do flip turns. She would stand and wait for me to swim toward her, and, instead of helping me, as soon as I reached the wall, she would push me as hard as she could, wildly, in different directions.

My shyness and inability to stand up for myself, combined with a lack of the right kind of shoes, clothes, and accessories my classmates all seemed to have, led to long, uncomfortable days at school where minutes were hours. My mother turned to my grandmother for help, sending me to stay with her overnight on weekends. This was how they saved me. Grandma didn't spend her days making spaghetti sauce from scratch, as did most of my Italian relatives. She bought it ready in a jar. We would eat store-bought raviolis and have long discussions, watch soap operas and baseball, and talk about her friends, all ladies in their sixties who caused her headaches and unthinkable inconveniences on numerous occasions. Watching her, I began to understand how to laugh easily, flirt, smile, and put an arm around a friend.

By the middle of my junior year in high school, I had become socialized. I learned it was okay, even necessary, to talk to people, and I became decent at it, even began to enjoy it. I had my first boyfriend. I cried as my parents and I drove away from my childhood home one fall day, my college bags piled into the trunk.

When writing my grandmother's eulogy, I begin to understand my childhood on a new level. Suddenly I am not sure whose isolation I am still feeling, my own or that of countless others who in some way or other feel different. As I try to recall the faces and situations of my classmates, Anne comes to mind. I stop what I am doing and find her company website online. She is a beautiful woman and her hair is wild and personable. A well of unspoken conversations move from a knot in my stomach, through my veins, and circulate in my mind, finally free. Was it hard to be one of the few black girls in our school?

Christine Ristaino   63

How could I have better understood her? What could I have done differently? Could we have earned each other's respect? How? There is a phone number on the web page, and I have a desire to call Anne and ask her these questions, but I don't.

Retrogression 14:
September 15, 2007, 10:12 p.m.

Ada and Samuel climb all over me and the plastic chairs at the store. The security guard gives me his card. We walk out the door and pass the bench where the attacker had been sitting only a few hours before.

Chapter 14: Italian Americans and American Italians

A colleague of mine describes an experience that occurred in her classroom. "A student on the first day of his beginning Italian course walked into my class and proclaimed, 'I'm Italian.' I've never understood this. What right does he have to say he's Italian when he doesn't even speak a word of it?"

I think back to my childhood. As an Italian American, I was told by my mother, father, grandparents, aunts, uncles, great-aunts, great-uncles, cousins, and my great-grandmother, that I was Italian and it was something to be proud of.

I motion for Antonia to sit. We have talked about this before, but I share my point of view once again. "When you are told over and over again that you are Italian, you believe it. It becomes part of your identity," I say.

"But you are living in the United States," she responds. "Isn't it obvious you are from here and not there? What right do Italian Americans have to call themselves Italians given most of them only know about an Italy that existed years ago?"

"But this history is part of the identity Italian American families hand to their children when they are young. Their children feel Italian," I say.

Antonia thinks for a moment. "But how can they feel Italian when they've never been there? How can they feel Italian when they don't even understand the language? I don't understand!" she finally says. "And I told my student this."

I laugh. "I hear you," I tell her. "But you're challenging his identity. You need to let your students down easily. From experience I can tell you, it's a shock."

As the daughter of two third-generation Italian Americans, I witnessed the struggle of Italian immigrants and their children firsthand. My great-grandparents were originally from Campania, in towns near Naples. Bernardino Lombardi, Maria Fidele Marinaccio, Carlo Ristaino, and Carolina Peppucci arrived with their families from Savignano di Puglia and Chiusano San Domenico in the late 1800s. They settled in Milford and Franklin, Massachusetts, quickly built homes, had families, and worked hard—my great-grandfathers building bridges and dams, my great-grandmothers running the family households.

To survive in the New World, my great-grandparents passed on their work ethic and love for family to my grandparents and then on to my parents. My father's identity wholeheartedly embraces his family—to talk about him without discussing his wife and children is nearly impossible, and the success or failure of his five children has everything to do with how well the family is doing and how he is feeling about himself.

"Do you want to know who I am?" he once asked. "Look at my children. That's who I am."

Every day of my childhood, I was reminded in some way (spoken or unspoken) of that magical land across the ocean my great-grandparents had left behind. All my relatives considered themselves Italian and said they were Italian. We made our own raviolis, homemade pasta, three-day sauce. We gathered every Sunday, ate, laughed, and drank together. I was convinced this was the way Italians behaved.

I was not curious about Italian culture when I went to Italy for the first time. I thought I knew all about it. But I wanted to experience my Italian origins in their purest, cold-pressed form. I was shocked when I heard from the Italians that I was not Italian. During my six-month stay in Italy, I began to wonder who I was. Often, people would pull their children closer to them when I walked by.

"Why are people afraid of me here?" I asked the family I was staying with.

"They think you're a gypsy," the mom said.

It was true. I had brought my best flowered skirts with me to wear in the hot Roman sun, and with my curly hair, I did resemble a gypsy.

I saw that Italian women knew how to dress well and were also aware of social rules I had never been exposed to before. I discovered most Italians now make a twenty-minute sauce and buy pasta from the store.

"You're more Italian than the Italians," one man said to me in Italy after having learned my family makes its own pasta from a flour and water base.

Antonia has a change of heart following a visit to Italy. "It has not been an easy transition," she tells me, "leaving Italy and moving here. I constantly feel torn. I often wonder where I belong. Sometimes I don't know who I am anymore. I feel Italian and yet when I go to Italy, I cannot accept the mindset that keeps us tied to a status quo. In America I have learned to dream big and expect rewards for my hard work. I am free to be who I want, and my friends and family tell me I've become

American. Italy is changing. So am I. But the Italian Americans have always wanted Italy to remain the same, to be that mythical land their parents and grandparents created for them. I know Italy is changing. Every time I return, I see it, and part of me wishes it wouldn't. I guess I have more in common with the Italian Americans than I initially imagined."

I think back to a day during my first weeks in Italy, when everything had gone wrong. I had wandered the streets of Rome, trying to clear my head, and found myself in a luggage store in search of a small bag.

"You can't buy here," the owner had told me. "This is not your type of store," he said, pointing to the door.

It was a few weeks into my first semester abroad in Rome, and I was wearing a flowered skirt, my curls falling against my neck. I left the store in tears, walking down ancient streets, feeling the weight of a history I didn't fully understand.

A woman touched my shoulder. "Americana?" she asked.

"Sì," I replied.

"America," she said and smiled, handing me a tissue.

Retrogression 15:

September 15, 2007, 10:11 p.m.

We finish our discussion with police officers and security. They look at me, warn me, "Change the locks when you return home. When a purse is stolen, they often come to your house to rob you again." The store manager gives my children Hi-C in red plastic cups.

Chapter 15: Barbs

Here is the other side of my family. We throw barbs at each other sometimes. It's great fun. We all love it, except my mom. To soften the game, my mother gushes and is overly kind. My family loves to laugh and joke, but occasionally the darts we throw stick where they shouldn't and aren't easily brushed away.

We are all vacationing at my parents' house in Maine. My brothers arrive on a Saturday, full of goodwill, with a Chuck-O beanbag game, beer, scotch, computers, iPods, and toys for my children. The beanbag game is a blast, but I'm terrible at it. No matter who I'm paired up with, we lose. Advice is shared. The jokes begin.

"Maybe you should try holding the whole bag in your hand rather than using just the edge," George wonders.

"Maybe you should get a new partner," Ernie advises him instead, chuckling to himself.

"I heard that," I say.

Later my father comments, "I'm noticing a pattern here. Whatever team Christine is on loses."

I hold it together for the rest of the game, but my father's comment hurts even though it wasn't meant to. I'm sure he's trying in his own way to reach me, get me to react, be more comfortable at our family gatherings. When I go inside, Ada is upstairs and won't come down. She's had a fight with her brother and doesn't want to talk.

"We don't have to talk if you don't want to," I say to her when I spy her hiding behind a chair. "Just sit with me for a while."

She climbs on my lap and I hold her. I can see by the shape of her face she feels relaxed, safe. I tell her how much I love her and tears come to my eyes and then they are falling one by one, but I'm really crying about the game and things I've never told my family.

My brothers don't realize I was raped at a young age by somebody I didn't know, nor that I was molested at an even younger age by somebody we all knew. As a result of these two events, distrust has crept into every corner of my life.

My husband and father can't understand why meat has to be cooked so thoroughly. My mother laughs at me when I flee from the cancer-causing chemicals she sprays on the table to kill germs. My father says I'm ridiculously paranoid when I want to replace the dead batteries in his fire alarm.

"We'll smell it if there's smoke here," he says. "What are the chances of a fire, anyway?"

But the chances of being molested, raped, or assaulted are higher than I ever imagined, and I'm willing to bet these odds extend to fire, salmonella, or cancer.

When I leave my parents' home at the end of our vacation, I tear up. When I say goodbye to my family, I feel empty. When I see my brothers' curly hair, their eyes, their sweet smiles, their profiles, and when Milo hums a bar to the song "Convoy" from the seventies and we all hum the rest, I know how special they are, what we've survived together, and how much I've survived without them.

Retrogression 16:
September 15, 2007, 9:50 p.m.

I step out of the ambulance and my husband reaches for my hand. He puts his arm around me; says nothing. He talks with my sister-in-law, Olivia, and I take in the rhythm of their words.

Chapter 16: Aikido

During my first class with him, Rutherford Sensei said his aikido sensibility had saved his life. He and his nephew were on a highway. He was driving. A truck swerved and became perpendicular to his car. The car almost went underneath the bed of the truck, but Sensei figured out how to drive into the small sliver of space that stood between them, and then into a safety zone, without panicking.

I can only liken one's first aikido lesson to awkward teenage lovemaking. You know there should be benefits, but you can't quite figure out what you're doing. I spent most of the first few lessons pinned beneath my classmates as they explained how to correctly complete the techniques.

I had taken five classes of aikido before I left for a family vacation. I had learned how to roll out of a sticky situation and could also awkwardly finish some of the moves. But upon my return, I felt just as lost as I had on the first day. As I struggled with one move after another, I wondered how long it would be until the techniques felt familiar and natural. It was at this point that the belt holding my aikido top in place became loose and unhinged. When it happened, I couldn't understand why my partner stepped away mid-move.

"Did I do something wrong?" I asked him.

"You lost your belt," said Rutherford Sensei, who had been observing us.

I looked down to see an open shirt, my brown bra, and a navel.

"Oh," I said. "I can't believe . . ."

But by this time, Sensei and my partner had begun to attack and effortlessly throw each other into a roll, one after the other with butterfly movements.

Before I left for vacation, we had been working on grabs. How do you destabilize a person enough so he or she loses balance and ends up on the ground? I discovered when I returned that we had finished grabs. We were now figuring out how to sidestep a punch. I was told to punch straight toward the person's face, but I was much shorter than my partner. I moved my hand upward, but stopped midway. The man I was hitting, a tall, muscular man, looked at me and waited.

"Go ahead," he said.

"But I don't want to hit you," I told him.

"I know you don't," he said. "None of us do. And you won't. I'm ready."

So I tried to hit him—four times to be exact. Each time he blocked, grabbed me, pivoted, and placed me gently on the floor, turning my arm just a smidge to give me a slight gnawing pain in my wrist. When I felt the pain, I would signal with my other hand that it had started to hurt.

Then he tried to hit me and I blocked. He talked me through it. "You make a triangle with your arms. Yes, that's right. Now you want to pivot and take me with you. One more step. Yes, now put me on the floor. Turn." His hand would go down and it would be done. Each time he punched toward me, I blocked. Every time I blocked, he told me how to bring him down.

Rutherford Sensei clapped and we returned to a kneeling position on the floor. As Sensei demonstrated and explained the next move, in my mind I compared the hand of the aikido student to the one that had come down on my face two months before. This man's hand was firm and purposeful. The other hand swung at me with no real direction. Contact with the aikido student connected me to him. Every second of this encounter, I felt looked after. With every second of the first one, I had felt more and more alone.

My next partner was a sturdy woman, only slightly taller than me. Again I was to hit her in the face and again I paused.

"Don't worry," she said. "I'll move away. It's okay."

I raised my hand and stopped.

"You can hit me," she said. "I'll move."

Mid-strike I stopped again. I couldn't do it. "I was attacked recently," I said. Tears filled my eyes. I wiped them as she tried to explain the move to me.

"Do you want to sit down?" she finally asked when I still stood there after the third explanation.

"No," I said. "I'll try. Could you explain once more?"

"Perhaps we can modify the move a bit. Here, you grab behind my arm and we won't do the first part."

Three moves and two partners later, I had stopped wiping tears and my nose on my *gi*. The loose, white robe had exposed me earlier, but now its towel-like material had absorbed everything.

Retrogression 17:
September 15, 2007, 9:30 p.m.

I can hear the children's voices, not their words but cadences, as they rise and fall. I imagine they are giving him a play-by-play of the attack and he is listening. I breathe in, not because the medic told me to do so, but because hearing my husband's voice allows me to.

Chapter 17:
Grief

I was in college, out for a drink with Emily. She had recently joined the swim team I was on, and I didn't know her well yet.

It was mid swim season and Saratoga Springs, New York, was cold and snowy. As Emily and I left the bar, the wind whipped the back of my neck. The house where I lived was far down the road, but Emily's room was only a block away.

"Let's go to my dorm," Emily said.

Emily and I ran as the wind seeped through our clothes, touching every part of us. We could see her building in the distance—institutional, pink, familiar. The hot air hit us as we entered. Our cheeks reddened. We walked into Emily's room, took off our coats, threw them onto a chair, and sat on her bed until heat moved into our bodies. The room spun. This was five months after I had been raped.

With the exception of a few school friends, I had barely told anybody. I leaned my head back onto her pillow and looked up at the low ceiling. I began to talk about the rape and what it had forced me to remember. For most of my life, I had ignored this event, pretended the day I had been molested had never happened. Sobs moved up my throat, filling the room with grief, rolling out of me in waves, one after the other. The next morning I woke, covered by a fuzzy blanket, Emily asleep next to me, her arm on my shoulder.

Retrogression 18:
September 15, 2007, 8:50 p.m.

The medics motion to me. I hear the fluency of nearby voices: my sister-in-law, Olivia; my Unitarian friends, Louise and Donna; my children. I strain to hear what they are saying. "We can't tell if your nose is broken. Any pain?" the medics ask. "Yes, and in the back of my head." "Yeah, you look like you've been banged up. You're going to have some bruises under your eyes. And you're pretty scratched up here around your shoulders." I stop listening, melt into the hard mattress, hear my children's voices and then a new voice, as familiar as the sun—my husband's.

Chapter 18:
The Parking Attendant

"We don't take credit cards," the man in the window said. I tried to place his accent and thought about the allergist's office I visited once a week for a shot. They took cards, I remembered.

"You don't?" I asked. "Lots of parking lots do."

"Well, we don't," he responded.

I had just finished visiting my doctor and it had gone well. It took less than an hour and I was relatively healthy.

"I only have a dollar and thirteen cents," I told him and handed him the dollar. "Do you mind if I go to the bank and return with more money?"

He sighed and looked at me, rolled his eyes, and finally said with an expression that didn't inspire any hope I would return, "Look. You owe me a dollar. Come back."

I drove away and found a bank machine, put my card in, and agreed to pay the machine fee for withdrawing money. "Insufficient funds," was the machine's response to my request. Well, I had known we were close this month.

I walked to my car and rifled through the ashtray, drink holders, CD compartment. I opened the trunk and lifted the items there one by one: a lifejacket with hearts on it, my son's *Polar Bear, Polar Bear* book, a folder, a huge poster of Italy, bargain-framed, and a diaper bag with pissed-on clothes in it from the day before. *I really need to take this bag inside*, I thought.

Exhaling, I stuck my hand into the bag and felt around for change, coming up for air with fifteen cents. I closed the trunk and walked slowly to the door on the driver's side. Then I got in and drove back.

I parked on the side of the road and approached the parking lot exit. There were two booths. *Which one was it?* I wondered.

I watched the two men in the windows as they worked. They both looked like the man I had spoken with. *Why can't I tell the difference between two black men?* I said almost out loud.

I was comforted only slightly by the realization that I don't distinguish well between blond girls either. *Is that any different?* I wondered as I waited for the men to look up. Why did the first oversight seem so much more offensive to me?

The man in the second booth recognized me. "You came back," he said and smiled, the first smile I had seen from him.

"Look," I said as I approached his booth. "It's the end of the month. I don't have it. I did find fifteen cents. I could give you my address and you could bill me."

"No, it's okay. Pay me the next time," he said and his eyes seemed to invite me closer to the window.

"Are you sure?" I asked, leaning in.

"It's okay. You're honest."

I said the words to myself. I'm honest.

I had known this about myself, but somehow, coming from him, it meant more to me now. I nodded, a long nod from somebody who was no longer a dollarless wretch, and walked to my car, feeling as rich as the prodigal son must have the day he returned home.

Retrogression 19:
September 15, 2007, 8:15 p.m.

I call two numbers from Louise's cell phone, the only two I have memorized in Atlanta. My husband's voice—I leave a message. "Hit in the face," "robbed," "we're okay," "kids weren't hurt," "Druid Hills and Briarcliff." Another to my sister-in-law, Olivia, who lives twenty minutes away. She arrives in seconds it seems. "My God, Christine. This is terrible," she says.

Chapter 19: Intuition

I had felt the darkness of the night engulf me as soon as I stepped out of my house. It swallowed me up, made me rush to my car, unlock the door quickly, and relock it just as fast. It was 11:00 p.m. on a Thursday night, and I was counting on using the drive-through to pick up a prescription I had dropped off earlier without ever having to leave my car. When I arrived at the pharmacy, I saw the drive-through was closed. *Shit*, I thought, and parked.

I was even more disappointed when I realized I had made the trip for nothing, since the pharmacy had closed at 10:00 p.m. I exited the store and walked on the sidewalk toward my car. I turned and there in front of me, inches away, stood a black man. I was propelled backward three steps. It was as though I had lost control of my body and something else had taken over my legs. The man stopped walking and stood to the side of my car. We stared at each other for what seemed like much longer than it should have been. Every cell in my body was aware of a potential threat, every cell alert and ready for a counterattack had there needed to be one.

A car pulled into the lot.

"I'm sorry," I said. "I didn't mean to do that."

Shaking myself out of my stupor, I walked past the man. Our bodies were inches apart as he slid by. I put the keys into the car door and watched him and the new arrivals enter the store. Once in the car, I turned on the radio and looked for a good song, trying not to cry.

The image of this man at the drugstore parking lot stayed with me into the next day. I couldn't shake him off. I was still feeling anxious when the doorbell rang that evening. My husband and I had friends coming for dinner, and although I had been preparing for their arrival all day, the bell startled me just the same.

Don, Joan, Mark, and I ate in the kitchen, and our five children were around a small table in the living room. I was still trying to shake off the strangeness that had enveloped me the day before when Joan began talking about a friend from work who was about to retire.

"They were having a big conference. All these people had been flown into Atlanta, and she didn't show up for a meeting, which is unlike her. Everyone was worried and they called her fiancé. He went to check on her and found her body on the apartment floor."

"She's dead?" I asked.

"Yes."

"And you used to work with her?" I said.

"Yes."

Joan is kind, intelligent, and introspective, but I especially admire her quiet strength. It's rare she talks about her personal problems. But now I could see she was struggling to keep her mind on anything else.

"I can't stop thinking about it," she said. "I keep wondering what it must have been like the last moments of her life."

"I'm so sorry, Joan. Are you okay?" I asked.

"Well, it was all by chance. He was with a realtor looking for an apartment. She had been walking her dog and she overheard them talking. She said, 'Don't forget my place.' She was selling her condo to move in with her fiancé. When the security guard called and asked if he should escort the man up, she had said no, explaining she didn't want him to think she didn't trust him because he was black."

I began asking inane questions of Joan. All the questions people had asked me after my attack came flooding back.

"What was she like?" I finally said.

"She edited some of my papers and she was the best editor in the world," Joan said. "She was always so trusting and, well, I think of that. She wanted to trust him, and there's a book about this, that humans don't listen to their gut feelings because they want to be nice. Because maybe deep inside something didn't feel right, but she didn't want to be prejudiced."

"Yes," I said. "We do disregard our gut feelings. But it's hard to know anymore when a fear is based on a gut feeling or a prejudice."

The room became silent. "I hate when people prove stereotypes right," I said, trying to fill the void and at the same time not communicating my idea well at all. "That's not what I meant. I hate it when people fit into a stereotype is what I wanted to say."

I thought of a conversation I once had with a student. "When I'm alone at night in my room and afraid, I imagine a black man breaking through my door, nobody else. It's as though the media has planted a black face in my head. That's all I see," she said.

The four of us sat, each in our own world. I began to wonder whether all black men feel as though they're viewed as potential rapists or killers. I had read an article about this by a black man who liked to walk the streets at night and would whistle classical music to put white New Yorkers at ease.

I thought of Joan's friend—middle-aged, successful, an important contributor to cancer research, someone who wanted to make the world better, about to move in with her boyfriend, happy—hit with a blunt object, dead. How differently my attack could have turned out had I hit my head harder on the pavement.

I could see my neighbor's house out my window, her television lights softly flickering, and imagined my house was made of glass. *Who else besides my neighbor can see in?* I wondered.

"Did they catch him?" I asked softly.

"Yes," Joan responded. "He came back to the apartment with some friends. He had wanted to steal more."

Later that night I couldn't sleep. I looked online at the *Atlanta Journal Constitution*. There she was. She was beautiful, competent, successful. I read about the man accused of killing her. He had been convicted before of theft, and suddenly I needed to find his picture. I pulled up article after article and finally, I found him. I looked at his photo. He was not the man who had robbed me. He was twenty-two, black, and handsome. Would I have trusted him?

I remembered the man at the drugstore, how something deep inside had screamed, *You aren't safe.*

I closed out the screen and put my laptop away. I wasn't sure anymore what I had been hoping to find or how to feel about any of this. Atlanta slept, people continued to murder, black men were accused of all kinds of crimes, and, on this particular night, I felt alone and unsettled—a sea of people and glass all around me.

Retrogression 20:
September 15, 2007, 7:32 p.m.

We are standing on the sidewalk in front of the store. A police car pulls into the parking lot. The officer gets out of his car and approaches us. Who is the victim? He turns and begins to ask me question after question. What did he look like? How did he strike? What was he wearing? How long did it last? What was in my purse? Were the children hurt? He writes everything on a pad of yellow paper. My children stand, planted next to me, uncharacteristically still.

Chapter 20: Eitan

E itan and I are driving five children under the age of seven to Edisto Island—a six-hour trip. A few days after we had put a deposit on a rental house for the two families to vacation together, both our spouses discovered they had to work until Wednesday of that week. On Monday evening Eitan and I pack up his minivan and head out.

Eitan is six foot five, even taller than my husband. He runs every day and is muscular and thin. He's dark—dark-eyed, tan-skinned, with black, short hair. He is always animated and his brown eyes reflect his mood. He is patient and kind to his children. Eitan is from Israel, and although he enjoys his life in the United States and has done very well—a top scholar in his field—he longs to return to his native country. He battles himself constantly since he is armed with the knowledge that moving back would most likely result in taking on a job with less prestige, a cut in pay, and a drop in his family's quality of life. Eitan might have a job offer in Israel, and he tells me this staccato, in between bathroom stops, children asking for juice boxes, battle cries from the seats behind me, and the buckling and unbuckling of my seat belt as I illegally jump from front to back, trying to soothe all five of them.

After two hours, we stop to eat a late dinner at a Wendy's. We are in Augusta, Georgia. I spend most of our restaurant break in the bathroom trying to clean my son, who has pooped all over himself. After what seems like an endless round of wiping feces off of his rear end, feet, ankles, lower back, and, yes, hands too, I take his pants and underpants, wrap them in paper towels, and throw them into the trash, replacing them with fresh clothes. While we are in the bathroom, the sky goes from a murky blue to black. Samuel and I enter the eating area as the kids busy themselves with fries and other unhealthy delights. Eitan and I speak about a strategy to get them back into the car, and I hand Samuel cold chicken fingers and fries already slopped in ketchup.

We put the children into a line at the door. Eitan holds his son, his youngest, in his arms and the hand of one of his daughters. My daughter and Eitan's oldest link arms and skip in unison behind Eitan. I carry my son and a purple bag full of backup clothes, wipes, and snacks to tide us over. As we approach the car, Eitan comments that the atmosphere outside the Wendy's is considerably different than when we went in. A van is parked next to ours, doors open and loud music playing. Our daughters begin to sway and move their hips, giggling and stepping on each other's feet, almost falling at one point into the three men by the van.

"Come on, girls," Eitan says with uncharacteristic impatience. "Let's get into the car."

As we buckle in the children, two more men walk past us and join the three who are talking, and other cars circle the parking lot, windows open, loud music, and animated voices.

"I don't like black culture here in the South," Eitan says under his breath as he snaps his son into his seat.

"Really?" I respond, jerking my head up, still fumbling with my daughter's belt. Eitan surveys our five children and then slides the door closed. I jump into the front seat next to him and he starts the car.

"Black culture in the South scares me."

"Why?" I ask.

"I don't understand it. I don't know what to do with it. It's nothing like I've ever seen before."

A few hours later we arrive safely. We unpack the car and our sleeping children and spend the next two days maneuvering beach trips, meals, naps, and children's movies.

When our spouses arrive, my husband and Eitan pick up the conversation about black culture over dinner. We sit around a table eating a delicious sausage and zucchini dish made by Eitan. The zucchini has soaked up the flavor of the sausage and it's just right. I have never tasted anything like it, and I try to remember exactly how Eitan made it as he describes our trip. "The ride was good," Eitan says. "But there was one moment that scared me. We were leaving the Wendy's in Augusta and the girls were skipping to the car, but really close to this van playing loud music. Only here in the South is there such a thing as black culture. Anywhere else you don't run into it. I've become more prejudiced because I've come face-to-face with black culture and I don't like it. It scares me."

Mark thinks about this for a moment and says, "When you live in a place like Seattle, you can be an idealist about race because there's not a big African American presence. But once you arrive in the South, it becomes real. You're faced with the good and the bad and you have to take a position."

"So you agree with me about black culture, then?" Eitan says.

"It's really not black culture at all," my husband responds. "It's a matter of economics. It's black and white poor culture. The kids you and Christine teach, for example, they are well off. They've had a support system. Christine won't admit what I'm talking about when I say that those students who the school classifies as average or below average usually don't have a strong support system. The black kids I teach at the advanced level, though, I think they have had to work harder to overcome things than most students. By the time they arrive at your doorstep, they've made it."

"I think what you are talking about is affirmative action," Eitan says.

"But this is the thing. This is why affirmative action works. There was a Vietnamese student who studied with me. I think she graduated valedictorian of her class, but at the time when I wrote her a recommendation letter, I didn't know this yet. I wrote three letters, in fact. Two were for students who were from upper class, wealthy families and they seemed fairly pampered by life, although it's impossible to tell for sure. This student of mine who was Vietnamese, she had to basically be the translator and the only link her parents had to this country. Without her, they couldn't communicate. She went on every shopping trip with them, helped them pay their bills, everything. She must have spent seventy percent of her time helping her parents survive. I wrote in my letter that she was one of the top three students of the school, but I would rank her the highest because of the obstacles she has had to overcome to get where she is. The other two students, well, they were from the upper class. Things had been easier for them. This is why I think affirmative action works."

We stand and begin to clear the table. Eitan continues, "Mark, you're an idealist, though, and idealists are what make affirmative action work. I had a black graduate student assistant when I first arrived here. She was horrible. She wasn't doing any of the work. I wanted to kick her out of the program, but when I met with her committee, they said it was nearly impossible. They all skated around the issue, but finally I got them to say it—it's because she was black. They told me I had to document everything, so I did. It took hours. Finally, we did let her go. Now will I hire another black student? Probably not. I have three children. I have to find grants to pay my salary. I am running from one thing to another every day and my kids crawl into bed with us each night. Do I have time to document? No. Now for an idealist like Mark, maybe he would have taken the time to help this black student get back on track. But I just don't have time for these things."

I try to ask Eitan if he thinks his uneasiness with black people might have affected the way he viewed this graduate student's work or affected her and how she worked for him, but Eitan responds that he wasn't the only person who had documented poor work habits. Soon my husband and he are onto another topic. My eyelids are heavy and I feel as though I've had a lobotomy. I have so much to say on this topic, but three days of parenting five small children has wiped every combination of words out of my head. After muttering a few unintelligible phrases to my husband and placing the last dish in the dishwasher, I kiss Mark on the cheek and go to bed. In the safety of twilight sleep, I can hear pieces of conversations: Hillary and Barack, Israel and Palestine, standardized testing in schools. The cadences of their language rise and fall as I struggle to keep my eyes open for just one more word.

Retrogression 21:
September 15, 2007, 7:15 p.m.

Donna calls somebody on her phone and I touch the tops of my children's heads. Soon there is a woman running toward us. She is running, yes, running. It's Louise from my congregation. I feel her body, warm and solid, surround mine. She stays there and hugs me.

Chapter 21: Did She Just Say That?

S ummer evenings in Atlanta are balmy, but the season was beginning to change and so it often cooled at sunset. One evening I found myself at Zivah and Eitan's house. Zivah is dear for many reasons, but one thing I particularly appreciate is that she throws the best children's birthday parties in the world—delicious Israeli dishes, enough food to feed the whole neighborhood, people from different ethnic backgrounds, music, and mayhem. Her approach to child-rearing mirrors the state of her parties—chaotic, passionate parenting. Zivah and I were on our way to meet a friend of mine for a drink at a local pub, but first we had to say goodbye to Zivah's family.

Zivah is a delight to watch with her children. She speaks to them in Hebrew unless I am there, and then she peppers her conversations with English for my benefit. When she leaves her house for a visit to the drugstore, a beer and a snack, or even a trip to the mailbox, it's as though she's going away for months.

The children gather around. There are embraces, sometimes even tears.

After a few goodbyes and false starts, we drove away. We fell into easy conversation, and when we arrived, a few minutes late, we saw that Camilla, an Italian friend of mine who worked at a college nearby, had saved us a table outside the restaurant. Camilla and Zivah had already met at my home, twice, and they both expressed interest in knowing each other better.

We sat and talked for over an hour and soon Camilla was leaning toward us, about to reveal a secret.

"You know," she said with a slight Italian accent. "You are really making me change my mind about Jews. Up until now I had a little bit of a problem. Just a little bit." As she said this, Camilla put up two of her fingers to show just how small.

I looked uncomfortably at Zivah. This was something I hadn't heard before from Camilla in the eleven years I'd known her.

She continued, "I was at this workshop and they asked us to talk about our prejudices. Well, I couldn't think of any and then I remembered—Jewish," she said in a sentence that was more Italian than English-sounding. "Two of my students were Jewish and I gave them a B+ and they wanted an A, but they didn't work that hard and I didn't want to give them an A. Then lawyers called me and said my students were going to sue me. So I had this prejudice against Jewish based on these two students. And I really didn't know any other Jews. But you wouldn't believe it, in this workshop guess who the two best friends I made were? Jewish!" she said.

Zivah and I listened quietly. Neither of us said much. After Camilla finished her story, I tried to tell them something funny about my son, but it came out sounding flat.

"I'm tired," Zivah said. "Could you take me home?"

"Sure," I said. We hugged Camilla. "Will you join us next week?" Camilla asked.

"Yes, I will," Zivah replied.

On the way home Zivah and I talked about her job, which suddenly seemed fraught with difficulty. At her house, Zivah said, "I had a great time. Thank you so much."

As soon as I arrived home, I called Camilla. I had felt Camilla's discomfort as we left the restaurant and I wanted to talk with her about what she had said. "Zivah didn't mention anything on the way home," I told her. "I don't think she's upset."

"I don't know. She became tired right after I spoke and she seemed unhappy. What do you think? Was what I said bad?"

"Well, I'm not sure I understood your message. I never knew you felt this way about Jewish people."

"But I don't. I love everyone. You know that," Camilla said.

It was true. Camilla did love everyone. She was always marching or fighting for a cause. She cooked for janitors and housekeepers to thank them for their help all year. She traveled everywhere so she could learn about new cultures. She was friends with everyone.

The next day Zivah called to ask me a question, but our conversation was stilted.

"Were you uncomfortable with what Camilla said last night?" I finally asked.

Zivah paused. "Yes, I was. Christine, I know Camilla is your friend, but I was upset and offended by what she said. I'm not joining you next week. I don't feel comfortable."

"Zivah, I know what it sounded like, but I think it came out wrong. I don't know what's going on. I'm going to talk to her about it again."

I called Camilla and she told me the story again, with the same outcome. Camilla didn't like Jewish people? It still didn't make sense.

"It just sounds as though you are saying you don't like Jews, but you met a few Jewish people recently who were nice. This doesn't sound like you at all," I told her.

"No," Camilla said. "I like everyone! It's not true I don't like Jewish people."

Camilla began to speak rapidly in Italian rather than English. In a passionate entreaty, she told me that when the workshop leader had asked them to discuss a particular prejudice they held, at first she couldn't think of a single one. Then she remembered how angry she was at these two students and decided she would focus on them—but they were only two students and she was angry at them because they had tried to sue her. Her feelings had nothing to do with the fact they were Jewish. It was a coincidence, but for the purpose of the workshop, she had grouped them together. The ironic thing about her grouping was that the two people she had befriended during the workshop happened to be Jewish.

I called Zivah, excited about my discovery, and Zivah's husband, Eitan, answered the phone. Zivah wasn't home, but Eitan brought up Camilla's conversation.

"I keep telling Zivah to let it go," he said.

"Eitan," I responded. "Something was lost in the translation. Camilla didn't communicate in English what she had wanted to say."

I told him a translated version of what Camilla had said in Italian.

"You know, Christine, I hear what you are saying, but deep down she probably doesn't like Jews and that's okay."

"No, Eitan," I said. "It's not okay to dislike Jews, but that's not the point. The point is I'm certain it was a misunderstanding."

"I'm not as optimistic as you are, Christine. But look, all of us are prejudiced. We should just acknowledge it and move on. It doesn't even mean we can't see Camilla and have a good conversation with her."

Zivah called me later. "I'm still upset," she said. "I'm not as sure about it as you are."

Camilla emailed Zivah, apologizing for the misunderstanding and asking if she wanted to have coffee and talk more about it, and Zivah responded, saying she'd like to, but they never did.

During a conversation months later, Camilla added a new complexity to our discussion.

"I don't think what I said about the students bothered Zivah at all, Christine," Camilla told me over lunch one day. "It was my comment about Palestine."

"What comment about Palestine?" I asked her.

"Do you remember? I told her I sympathized more with Palestine than with Israel. Zivah didn't respond, but I think that's what upset her."

"Camilla, I don't remember that part of the conversation at all."

"Maybe you were too focused on what came before. You know, I have a friend. She's from Israel, too, but she feels the same way as I do about Palestine. She was really bothered by the Israeli bombing of the Gaza Strip last December. I don't think I'm going against Jewish people or Israelis, just policy decisions I don't believe are fair. But I'm glad I said this to Zivah, even if it did upset her, because it's what I believe and we all should say what we believe, don't you think?"

"Yes," I replied.

I showed Zivah what I had written about our evening with Camilla.

"Christine," she said. "You remembered this conversation so differently than I did. Camilla's words about Jews were more harsh than what you wrote. And like you, I don't remember anything about Palestine coming into the conversation."

Perhaps, I admitted to myself, I had made Camilla softer than she had sounded, closer to the image I had of her. Zivah had prefaced her comments by telling me how much our friendship meant to her. Then her words tumbled out with urgency, as though I had missed something vital about her.

Retrogression 22:
September 15, 2007, 7:10 p.m.

I hug Ada to my side. Samuel rubs my cheek with his hand. Donna from my Unitarian congregation walks in our direction from the parking lot. I wave. I had just said goodbye to her— how long ago? Minutes? Hours? Days? She begins to smile and then changes expression midstream. "What happened?" I don't know—can't put it into words. "We were just mugged—or assaulted. I'm not sure." "Are you okay?" Donna drops down past my face and kneels in front of my daughter. "Are you all right, Ada?" she asks, wiping away Ada's tears.

Chapter 22: Cartoons

I attended a presentation given by Ronnie Bonner, Senior Vice Provost for Diversity and Community. I had seen his name everywhere but had never met him. In person he was dynamic and intense.

Part of the provost's presentation involved a recent incident, where a student—who had lived in Israel twice before—had published a cartoon in the university's student newspaper that seemed to equate Israel's security wall with Nazi imprisonment and the persecution of Jews in Poland. "I feel there are some eerie similarities between the boundary wall erected in Jerusalem and the walls of the Jewish ghettos in Europe during World War II. . . . I have no intention of inciting a connection with the Holocaust," he had written, despite having just done so.

The campus began an involved debate culminating in a letter written by fifteen of the university's most prominent, tenured professors, condemning the cartoon and asking the newspaper for a public apology for having printed it.

The provost wanted to know what tone this type of letter set for students and if a different approach could have included rather than alienated students from the conversation. We all agreed—there were charged topics, topics that made incredible pain resurface. How could faculty, despite the pain the cartoon had provoked, have reached out to this student?

After the discussion, I approached Provost Bonner. "My children and I were attacked in a parking lot, and people kept asking me if my attacker was black. My angry responses to their questions stopped our conversations."

The provost nodded.

"When something is painful," I said, "you just want to shut down, stop a conversation, prevent it from happening. It's sort of a protection. But I was alienating people."

I told the provost about my son's fears of black men after the attack. "I wanted to recognize this was a fear based on an experience, but I also wanted to diffuse it."

After our conversation, the provost shook my hand and thanked me for talking with him.

When I walked away, I felt great. I had shared how his story had affected me. But later that night, I couldn't sleep. I wondered if I had gone too far, talked too much, taken advantage of the provost's willingness to listen. Did he think I agreed with my son about fearing black men? Did he feel singled out as a black man? Had I conveyed what I wanted or had I rushed through the story, not connecting the dots, my message that I was appreciative of the risks he was taking lost somewhere? And was this topic just too painful? I had taken a risk, one I would continue to take, but the lines still remained dizzying.

Retrogression 23:

September 15, 2007, 7:09 p.m.

I stand on the sidewalk in front of the store. Next to me in an awkward line are Ada, Sam, an Asian couple with a baby, and a white woman. I wipe my face with napkins, guess at where the blood is. Nobody tells me for sure, and I use Ada's tears to wet the paper. A woman exits the store and asks what happened. "I have been inside the store for about an hour," she tells us. "That man was on the bench when I arrived."

Chapter 23: Misunderstanding

When I help my children wash in the bathtub, I am careful. I put shampoo on my hands and massage their scalps. I soap up their backs, arms, legs, hands, and feet. When I get close to their privates, I hand them the soap.

I explain to my daughter and son, "If anyone touches you in your private parts, anyone, you tell me or Dad. You promise?"

When my son refuses to wash himself after pooping in his pants, I ask him first, "Can I wash you?" and when my daughter soils her pants after a bout of the runs, I inquire hesitantly, "Do you mind if I help you clean up?"

I ask these things because I know how much is at stake. I think back and try to remember what my mother did—if she washed me in my private places, or asked me before she did, but nothing comes to mind. I remember her sweet smile, her laughter, her songs, but I don't know who washed me when I was five.

When I think of the man, I try to turn the story into a mistake. I try to imagine it was a misunderstanding—like when a parent washes a child in his or her private places and perhaps that child remembers incorrectly. Could that have happened? I worry about this scenario every time I have to wipe off my children's poop or help them wash up, but deep inside I know what I remember was more than a misunderstanding.

Retrogression 24:
September 15, 2007, 7:07 p.m.

A woman with brown hair in her mid-thirties arrives. "Oh my God," she says and throws her arms around me. "Oh my God. Are you okay?" My daughter calls my name and I touch her hand. "It's okay," I say, lifting my son from the cart and pulling him into my chest. "We're okay." "It's not okay, and you're not okay," she says. "I saw it."

Chapter 24: Samir and His Wife

Damn immigrants don't know how to drive. What the hell did you do? Fucking immigrant! You asshole. Why don't you go back to where you came from!

—A quote by a police officer to Samir, after a cement truck hit his car.

At the Unitarian Universalist congregation, you can generally find fifteen or so children whose parents insist they attend a religious education (RE) class in the summer. On this Sunday, however, because the sermon would be given by activist Reverend Joseph Lowry, there were over fifty children between the ages of five and twelve who needed to be accommodated into RE classes. "Please could you stay and help with the children?" one administrator had asked me.

I wanted to hear Lowry speak, but the children pulled me in their direction, too. "Okay," I replied.

There were too many children to hold class, so we took them outside to the playground. It was here where I had a long conversation with Samir's nine-year-old son, who told me about a recent trip to Alaska he had taken and showed me photos of a cousin from India, which were on his new iPod. "I don't have a single picture of my sister," he said. "I'm going to have to change that."

I first met Samir at my university. I often ran into him in the parking lot in the mornings. Always afraid I would make a mess of his name, I rarely said it, or when I did, I would speak it quietly under my breath. Samir always remembered my name, and he pronounced it as though it were the title of a great piece of literature.

The day I took Ada to aikido for the first time, I recognized Samir right away.

"I didn't know you did aikido," he said to me. "Is she here for the class?"

"Yes," I said. "She's new. We're both new."

"Well, I'm her teacher," Samir said. "This is my other life."

He took my daughter into his protective care, and I watched from the sidelines as she began her relationship with aikido.

After the service on the playground, Samir and I greeted each other and then his wife arrived. I had met her a few times, but I couldn't remember her name. She wasn't a practicing aikido member, but she sometimes brought her children to classes and her smile relaxed me.

"Have you met Christine?" Samir asked.

"Yes, I have," she said.

"Did you know she works with me?"

"I didn't," she responded.

"Your children are great at aikido," I said to her.

"My daughter sometimes doesn't want to go. But we told our children they have to take it forever so I will feel confident they are safe, or at least until they are ten," she said, laughing.

"Our daughter's so small," Samir added.

"I enrolled my daughter without asking her. But Ada likes it," I said.

"I've never done it, but it seems organic, somewhat grounding. The world's so fragmented," Samir's wife commented.

"It is. My children and I were attacked recently. That's why we started. I thought it would make all of us feel less vulnerable, but what I didn't count on was how connected it would make us feel to others."

"I didn't know," Samir's wife said and paused. "I've never been attacked. But there were some close calls. Like the time I was gardening and these two teens came into my backyard, grabbed my hands forcefully, and said, 'Get in your house, lady.' I did this thing where I lifted my hands up, opened them away from each other, and freed myself." Samir's wife showed me what she had done.

Samir clasped his hands in front of him. "She did an aikido move and she doesn't even know aikido. Isn't that amazing?"

"Then I screamed at the top of my lungs, with all the force I could gather. It's not natural to scream. In fact, it felt counterintuitive. But it worked. They both ran away so fast. When I got my bearings, I yelled after them, 'I could be your mother. I could be your sister. What were you thinking?'"

"Tell her about that other time in New York City—you know, that guy near the apartment building," Samir said.

"Oh, well I was walking home one night and there was this man waiting in a recessed doorway. We were both under a long scaffolding in New York City where they were doing work on the building. So once you entered, there was nothing you could do but go on. He had his hands folded in front of him. He stared at me. I didn't know what to do. So I asked him, 'Is this the way to Fifth Avenue? It is, isn't it?' I really thought he was going to mug me, but it completely disarmed him."

"I wish I could think that fast. Samir, has aikido made you more like your wife?" I said, laughing.

"Yes," he responded. "And I think it's also changed the way I react to people. One time I was in a terrible accident. My car was hit by a cement truck, and it turned around and around and slid into oncoming traffic. A few minutes after the accident, a policeman opened my door and began screaming at me about being an immigrant and my driving skills, as though being hit by a cement truck had been my fault because of who I am. I stayed calm and said, 'Look. I was just in a really bad car accident and I'm a bit shaken up, so could you give me a moment to collect my thoughts?' The man stopped yelling at me."

For a moment we were all silent. I glanced at my children. Samuel was inside a plastic house, calling out to Ada, "Hey Ada, look at me. I'm in the window."

Ada held on to the monkey bars, grabbed one bar, then the next, and acknowledged her brother with a nod.

"That's the worst story of them all," I told Samir.

I began to shred a paper napkin that was in my hand and thought about the implications of Samir's story. "The man could have shown compassion," I said. "Did you report him?"

"I did. There was a black officer who came after and I told him about it. But he said, 'There's nothing we can do.' He'd seen him do this before and it didn't end well when the person complained."

Samir shook his head and his whole posture changed.

I glanced again at my children. They had been talking with a boy about who would use the tire swing. "Mom," my daughter said when she caught my glance. "He's not sharing."

"I saw you talking with him—you and Sam. Why don't you talk more until you figure it out. I'll wait. We have time."

Retrogression 25:
September 15, 2007,
7:06 p.m. and 30 seconds.

"I was just attacked," I tell the Asian couple with the baby. "I need you to call the police." I'm not sure if they speak English, but then the man takes his cell phone out of a pocket and holds it out to me. "Please, could you dial?" I say, glancing at my hands, which are covered in blood. "I don't want to get blood on your phone."

Chapter 25: Waiting for Repairs

As most people in the United States began preparing emotionally for the seventh anniversary of 9/11, I was preparing for 9/15, the first anniversary of my own attack—so much so I was surprised to hear the radio announcement one morning to mark the 8:46 a.m. moment of silence when the first plane hit.

I had been feeling the weight of my own attack as August turned into September. In fact, everything had seemed more difficult. Even the small task of returning an email had become overwhelming. My son and I suffered from the same insomnia and often kept each other company in the early hours, and I couldn't help but acknowledge a feeling of restlessness that was getting worse as the fifteenth approached. It was around this time my son poured a full glass of water onto my computer. "Hey, Mom," he said, and when I looked, he tipped the glass over.

My husband and I try to support local businesses, so I took my computer to a Middle Eastern man who had his own store at a shopping center near my home. He was a small man who looked as tired as I felt.

He must have children, I thought.

"Your son poured water on your computer?" the repairman asked.

"Yes, on purpose," I said.

"Oh. I'll order some new parts," he said, touching the side of his brown hair. He wore glasses and his pupils shone from behind them, adding a seriousness to his expression. "It will take at least a week."

A week later I stopped by the shop unannounced to ask about my computer's progress. There it was, spread out in front of us like a jigsaw puzzle.

"I'm sorry," the store owner said as he fumbled in front of me. "I had to take your computer apart entirely. I usually work on IBMs and it's easy to change the keyboard on an IBM laptop. You just snap it in. But with Macs, you have to take the whole laptop apart." He frowned. "Look. Here's what I needed to take apart," he said, as he pointed to the frame. "See. Right here's the new keyboard." He slid his hand along the side and looked up. "And I've checked every key, but one of them doesn't work. See, this one right here. The caps lock." He touched the key with his finger and pressed it, even though it wasn't connected to a computer. "That one's not working at all. Every other key is working but this one." He looked at me and shrugged with half a frown. "I've asked them to send me another keyboard and they are going to, but it will be a few more days until it arrives."

"So when do you think it will be ready?" I asked.

"Three or four days. I will call you when it's ready."

"Okay," I said. "I'll see you in a few days."

I walked out of the computer store with my heart racing. A month earlier, one of the computer support techs from my university had fixed a problem with my computer. I thought I was going to have to bring my laptop to him. Instead, we both logged on under different names—he from campus, I from my house. I was amazed that both of us could move the mouse, type, and control what happened on the desktop. This experience had unnerved me. What else were people capable of doing and who else could do this? I thought of my computer, completely open and vulnerable on the countertop of a stranger's shop. I imagined insanely he was part of a terrorist organization and had decided to use my computer and email account to make plans. I would be arrested for suspected terrorist activities.

"But I don't know anything about this," I would say.

There would be a whole pile of emails sent from my account as evidence, and I would be led out of the courtroom, condemned to death. I'd wave goodbye to my husband and crying children, never to see them again. Or worse, I'd simply disappear and nobody would know where to find me. My family would search everywhere. I'd end up at Guantánamo Bay, no court date in sight, unprotected by the Geneva Convention, and with no way to contact those I loved for help.

I have to say, this scenario bothered me. Hadn't I felt connected to the computer repairman's tired eyes only a week before? I was disappointed in myself, but I couldn't stop worrying. I tried to quell the feeling of unease that kept tugging at me from inside, but this did nothing to prevent me from thinking something terrible could happen to us at any moment. The more I tried to put the scenario out of my mind, the more I thought of it. I didn't dare tell anyone. They would think I was crazy.

One night my husband and I had just put the kids to bed. It was late, and I could tell by the way my body felt, my arms stiff, my toes trying to poke through the hole they had found in my sock, that falling asleep would be an accomplishment. Perhaps this was why I decided to broach the subject of the computer repairman with my husband, against my better judgment.

"This man who is working on my computer. Why did he have to open it up so completely?" I asked as I filled the teakettle with water and placed it on the burner. "Don't you think it would be easy to change the keyboard? It's right there on top of the computer."

"Maybe it's attached to something inside," my husband said as he pulled two cups from the cupboard in front of him and placed teabags into them—chamomile for me, Irish Breakfast for him.

"And I don't understand this thing about the caps lock key. Does that sound strange to you?"

"Sam did pour a whole glass of water on it. I'm surprised there's not more damage."

"But what if he's doing something to my computer? What if he's . . . I don't know."

My husband frowned. He wasn't getting it. The scenario I had imagined had never even crossed his mind. The kettle whistled and I began to fill both cups with hot water.

"The tech people at my school. They could get onto my computer from campus. Do you think this man can do that?"

"I don't think so, honey. I think he's probably tired of looking at your computer. He's had it for almost two weeks," my husband said.

"I guess I'm afraid he's going to use my email account to plan something."

I took a sip of my tea and felt the sting of hot water on my lip. Should have waited. By the look on my husband's face, I knew he thought I had gone totally bonkers. Then we both began to laugh.

"What are you afraid of?" he finally asked. "Are you afraid he's a terrorist or something?"

The room was quiet. I sat at the kitchen table and tried to find its surface, which was obscured by bills, my daughter's homework, a few napkins, and a jar of honey.

"It's not just the computer repairman. I'm afraid of men. A white man at a gas station is a serial killer. A black man at night is a rapist. When I look around me, I'm so scared. Inside my head I know this doesn't make sense. But I'm afraid and I don't know what to do. Everywhere I look, there are images of scary men—on TV, the news, even on the Cartoon Network."

My husband nodded. "It's normal to be afraid of men after you've been attacked by one," he said.

"I know, but I'm afraid in general. I can't stand the idea of being separated from you and the kids. I worry they'll be kidnapped from their windows by construction workers, like that girl in Utah. And some people are thrown in jail for something they didn't do. And I could lose you in a car accident or something. And heart attacks. Toxic chemicals, hormones in chickens, everything is dangerous. And tomorrow is September fifteenth."

"It'll be all right," my husband said. "We'll be okay. You'll see. The fifteenth will come and go."

We finished our tea and walked up the stairs. I checked on the children before joining Mark in our room. The fear I had been holding onto all week seemed different than before. It had transformed into relief. I curled into my husband's back and let the softness of sleep take over.

When the man from the computer shop called again, I strained to hear his name over the phone but couldn't make it out. He told me that despite installing another keyboard, he still couldn't get the caps lock key to work. "I'm so sorry," he said. "Do you want me to try another one?"

"It's okay," I told him. "I don't really use the caps lock much. I appreciate all the work you've done to fix it."

I drove to the store and he showed me the caps lock key. My computer was all back together and it had a shiny new keyboard. I touched the man's hand. "Thank you for all the attention you gave it. Sorry it was such a bear."

He smiled. "It's okay. That's my job. Come back again," he said. I nodded. I would.

When I reached my car, I glanced back at the store. I could still see the computer repairman standing in the entrance, looking out, at me and at the world. From this distance, his smallness overwhelmed me. Was he as afraid of people as I was? Did 9/11 shake him up? Did it force him to wonder how he would make it in a world that no longer trusted him? I thought about his family. Did he have children? Were they at school like mine? How did they maneuver the changes taking place in their world? I sat in my car, thought about the computer repairman, and longed to ask him these things.

Retrogression 26:
September 15, 2007, 7:06 p.m.

I look around the parking lot, but I don't see anyone. A young Asian couple exits the store. The woman carries a baby and the man follows them. "Please help me," I say. They look at me and my children while Ada sobs and I bleed. "Help us," I say again. The woman pulls her baby closer to her chest.

Chapter 26: My Work

E ach day is more of a struggle. I hear an advertisement for a study about depression on the radio, and I fill in the blanks from there: trouble sleeping, overwhelmed by the simplest of tasks, difficulty concentrating, inability to focus, fear of dying at any moment.

"I'm depressed, my son doesn't sleep, and I think the two are connected," I tell my program director later on.

She is relieved, puts her hands on her lap.

"You've been having trouble focusing lately," she says. "I can handle it if I know you're depressed and you will eventually go back to being your old self again."

But even as she says this, I can barely remember what it was like to be my old self, a woman so focused on everybody else's needs and feelings that she didn't know what was important to her. I keep silent and we begin to plan for a leave of absence.

At home my son becomes increasingly agitated. He won't sleep. He's constantly afraid of bad guys creeping into his room at night, or bad guys following me around while he's at school, or bad guys chasing us through crowded stores or parking lots. I am not sleeping, and with each passing day, I become more and more anxious, to the point where, even when my son doesn't wake up as I carry him from my bedroom to his and place him into his bed, I have difficulty winding down, drawing the anxiety out of my chest. I begin to breathe, in and out, in and out, and I wonder how I will gather enough energy to teach in the morning, grade essays, or put the kids to bed the following night. I think, *What would it be like if all the professors at my university knew of my problems?* I have only told a few people about the attack on my children and me, and I imagine some of my female colleagues may have even experienced something similar. Perhaps we could have coffee and they could tell me what they did to heal.

Instead, we don't go beyond the superficial.

"Hi," I say when I pass my colleagues. "How are you?"

"Fine," they reply and smile.

I am fine, too, and perhaps they, like me, are carrying some unseen weight, but I never notice it, so carefully hidden.

"I want more," I say to my friend over coffee one day. "I want to reach out to my colleagues. They are interesting. I like them."

But as my despair deepens, I can't bring myself to say anything to them.

And soon my husband sits next to me on our bed. He has just read one of my stories from this book, a scenario that ends with me almost driving away with my son's car door open. He is disturbed by this ending and takes in a deep breath. "Where are you?" he says to me.

"Right here. Right here in front of you," I reply.

"What do you think of every day when you leave the house?" he asks. "Where do you go in your mind? Because I'm worried about you and the kids' safety when you drive."

"I'm okay," I answer. "Really, although I'm having trouble focusing and everything at work just seems so overwhelming. And I'm tired. And you must be, too, because of Samuel. Because I wish he would sleep."

And suddenly I am crying.

It's at a party, a few days later, when I decide to tell a colleague what happened to my family a bit over a year to the date after it occurred, for she has asked me about my research. As I describe this book, I admit that since the attack my family hasn't been the same.

"Why didn't you tell me?" she asks.

"I don't know."

"But we could have talked about this," she responds, reaching out her hand.

Her simple gesture is a gift.

I visit the chair of my department, a woman who teaches upper-level French classes. She has a rich sense of humor and deep blue eyes. I ask her how to apply for a leave and find myself recounting every detail, every last personal detail about my family—my son's sleeping problems, my anxiety and inability to focus, my husband's comments about the car door, our chaotic, unkempt lives. She hears every word.

"I'm so sorry you've had to deal with this. I had no idea how much this experience was affecting you and your family."

She writes emails to the dean's office and secures a spring semester off for me. For the first time in months, I feel relief.

There is a conversation I have yet to maneuver, for I desire communities of support all around me. I need the people I work with to know right away when I have been attacked or hurt. I want them to embrace my children, to ask me how they are feeling, how they are coping with the numerous challenges that life is bound to bring their way. And I would like to be there for them, to hear about their relationships, their research, and

Christine Ristaino 123

countless other day-to-day lost details. But how can I expect them to talk to me if I stay quiet? And what do I do with those who just want me to go back to the way I was, even though that seems impossible now?

Retrogression 27:
September 15, 2007, 7:05 p.m.

Although the night is warm, I begin to shiver. My legs are unsteady as I push myself up from the pavement. I don't look at my children as I try to find something to cover my face and absorb the blood pouring from my nose.

Chapter 27:
Pandora's Box

My friend Sarah emails an article to me on sexual abuse. Most victims don't experience trauma when they are being abused, it says. It's only later, when they realize what happened, that's the moment when it becomes traumatic. The less violent the experience and more trustworthy the abuser, the more trauma and guilt the person feels later on in life, as though somehow this former child had brought it on.

I close the article on my computer and call Sarah. As a child, she experienced abuse similar to mine. Her sister had been sexually abused over and over again by a friend of the family, but this same man had left my friend alone, almost. "He abused me only once," she tells me. "We went into a side room and he said, 'What's this?' and pulled out his penis. Then he grabbed my crotch and tried to touch me. I knew something bad had happened, but I worshiped this man." Sarah takes in a breath and then continues. "My sister experienced the same thing tons of times, and I know there are different levels to this, but what people don't understand is that it's all traumatic. It all counts. Abuse is abuse. It can happen one time or hundreds, but once it happens, none of us are ever the same."

The week I receive the article, I am also confronting another Pandora's Box. My university is going through growing pains. A community of graduate students camped out and protested on the quad for a number of days in support of cafeteria workers' rights to a union, equitable pay, and job security, and when negotiations broke down and they wouldn't leave, the university had seven of them arrested.

I hear about it from my students and am immediately upset. The university has a strong reputation for its ability to resolve issues through conversation and I am bothered by its reaction to peaceful protest. I sign a petition expressing discomfort at student arrests, remembering my father's arrest years before when he fought for women's rights to maternity leave at his school.

At a meeting I am introduced to some of the petition organizers and one of the graduate students who had ended up in jail. It is a small gathering; only four other people are there. The graduate student seems shaken, nervous, exhausted. He tells us about his experience and conveys appreciation for the petition in circulation. The faculty at the meeting plan to turn it in the following day. Later that night I email the graduate student, recount my father's experience in jail, and tell him he's brave.

As a result of the petition, the administration agrees to hold a forum the following Wednesday. When I arrive, the auditorium has almost completely filled with faculty, students, and staff. I sit next to the vice president of the university, a tall man with glasses and a bow tie. On a number of occasions, he has been kind to me and shown incredible compassion, and while sitting next to him at the meeting, I am reminded of his kindness. He had been there during the arrests and had warned students that if they didn't leave, there would be consequences.

I take notes on the president's response to faculty questions. His comments and the discussion that follows fill in gaps. I try to understand both the arrest and the underlying conflict. But the more I learn, the more confused I become. I am moved by a faculty member who expresses, with tears in his eyes, his disappointment that the issues leading to the protest had not been addressed quickly enough. I am also moved by the president's apology, which is full of possibility. He says that steps were being taken to address concerns but wishes in retrospect he had moved faster.

Outside the auditorium I speak to a dean and then a graduate student. Both are unhappy with the results of the meeting for opposite reasons. I write to the graduate student, saying it's important to take stock of what has gone right—the conversation has moved beyond graduate students and administrators. The whole university has met to talk about the issues he's fighting for.

That night as I put my children to bed, I can't shake a knot of despair that has settled in my chest. In my room I change into sweatpants and a loose shirt. "Mark," I say, when my husband comes into our room a few minutes later, "I'm having trouble understanding what really went on. I don't think the students should have been arrested, but I don't understand everything else—what happened, how it happened, when. I admire the grad students' courage, and I'm bothered they spent a night in jail. But my university seems to be taking steps to address the problem."

The room is quiet.

"I feel so terrible right now," I say.

"Why?" Mark asks.

"Because I can never take an unequivocal stand on anything. Everything always seems so complex. When I saw the video of student arrests, my heart broke for them, but I also felt for the vice president who had to make the call. I'm sure it was awful for everyone."

"But that's what people love about you. You're fair. You have compassion."

"But I want to be like my father—go on strike, stand strong for what I believe in. Instead, I just feel guilty," I say.

The word "guilt" reminds me of the article I had read a few days before. I go to my computer and begin to read it again. It describes me in a way I had not understood a few days before. The man who had abused me—my narrative was that it was my fault. I had asked him to scratch my back. Then, when he did more, I didn't stop him. I spent a lifetime seeing other sides to this issue, seeing the man my family loved—a kind man, a funny man, a great storyteller, a fantastic cook. What would they think if I told them he was also a child molester? For years I had imagined how they would feel. I imagined every hurt feeling, every doubt, every bit of anger turned back onto me, as though in telling my family, I would be the one who had betrayed them, not him.

This same scene plays out over and over again, becomes every scenario, every interaction. Other perspectives crowd out my own, and I become attached to each one, play out each situation, become each person involved. How can I take action when the possibility of betraying even one person is always so thick in the air. But being careful and not telling people my perspective has made me invisible. In the days that follow, I make a promise to myself. Before I open Pandora's Box and take on the pain and sorrow of the world, I have to understand unequivocally how each situation makes me feel.

Retrogression 28:

September 15, 2007, 7:04 p.m.

I will always think of my children's faces when I remember this crime—open mouths, hands cradling their cheeks, eyebrows furrowed like old people with permanent grooves, eyes exaggeratedly open. It is seeing their reaction that makes me understand what I failed to grasp on my own. He has beaten me up in front of them.

Chapter 28:
Seduced and Abandoned

I t's my turn to show a movie for the Italian program and I've chosen *Sedotta e Abbandonata* (Seduced and Abandoned). When I was in my late twenties, I loved this film. I must have seen it at least six times. It's a 1964 comedy directed by Pietro Germi, and it's all about Sicilian honor.

Because of its location in the Mediterranean, Sicily was dominated by every foreign power imaginable over the course of its long history—Greeks, Spaniards, Turks, Ostrogoths, Arabs, Normans, Bourbons, you name it. Once Italy was unified in 1871, it wasn't long before the Mafia took over in Sicily. But throughout this long occupation of powers, the Sicilians maintained control over their honor. It's still something they ferociously guard.

The Sicilian obsession with honor drives this film as Vincenzo Ascalone works to return honor to his family after his daughter, Agnese, becomes impregnated by her sister's fiancé. The family stages kidnappings, gunfights, serenades, and shouting matches, all to right this wrong and bring respect back to the family name.

When I arrive at the showing room, students spill over the seats and into the aisles. I stand in the front of the room, pop open the case, and slide the DVD into the player. As I introduce the film, I talk about Sicilian occupation and honor, and end by telling the students that this is one of my favorite Italian films.

I sit in the front, ready to be entertained. I watch the seduction scene, where Agnese and her sister's fiancé do it in the washroom while the rest of the family takes an afternoon nap. But Peppino Califano begins to treat Agnese poorly immediately afterward and he continues to do so throughout the film. I find myself cringing each time Agnese's father, Vincenzo, slaps his daughter and calls her a whore for her part in this misadventure, and I struggle to calm my anger when she is locked inside a room, away from all men except her brother, and has to bang on a pipe each time she needs to use the bathroom.

The part of the film that draws the most laughter involves a scene where Agnese's father and Peppino's parents stage a very public kidnapping of Agnese, part of their attempt to force their children to marry. But they kidnap Agnese's sister by accident. When they realize she's the wrong sister, they drop her on the side of the road. She sits sobbing while Agnese is taken away in a car. I used to love this scene, but now I find it hard to watch. What kind of a family would do this? I want to stand and apologize to my students, but they are too busy watching the film and laughing at the parts of the movie I used to love.

It's almost ten when the film is over. I slink to the podium and dismiss everyone. A few of my students stay to talk. I discuss some of the things that trouble me about the story. They listen but assure me the film had been a good choice.

Retrogression 29:

September 15, 2007,

7:03 p.m. and 20 seconds.

From the ground, my eyes follow the wheels of the cart as they circle up from the black tar. I can see Ada, with her hands over her face, sobbing, and Samuel's wide eyes just staring. I have never before seen eyes so wide.

Chapter 29: Falling Up

I'm almost late for a meeting and it's high-traffic time on campus in between classes. Fortunately, the building where I need to be is next door. I'm carrying a book bag filled with papers, my wallet, and an apple-and-cheese combination from Starbucks. I begin to run. There's a small, cement ledge where people often sit between the two buildings, and I decide to take a running leap so as not to break my stride. My bag is too heavy though, and I'm too old for this. Despite these things, I almost make it. Only my foot hits the cement ledge, but it is enough to send me flying through the air. My shoe decides to go in a different direction and lands feet away, next to an onlooking student. I break my fall with one hand. The other is too caught up in the handles of my book bag to be of any use. I find myself lying on the ground surrounded by people. Professors I know come to my rescue, holding papers that have flown from my bag. A hand lifts me. A student arrives with my shoe. I am bleeding only slightly—a small scrape to my wrist. I stand and smile.

"Are you okay?" somebody asks.

"Yes," I reply.

Everyone is relieved and then one person says, "That was one of the best falls I've ever seen. What would you rate it, a ten?"

"Well, maybe a nine and a half," his friend replies.

"No, an eight and a half," someone else concludes.

Suddenly everyone is rating my fall, including myself, and I am surrounded by people, definitely late for my meeting now, but I no longer care.

Retrogression 30:
September 15, 2007,
7:03 p.m. and 10 seconds.

My body lies on the ground, disengaged from my eyes and nose, which are taking in everything around me—the smell of blood and tar, old cigarettes, a loose-leaf paper folded on one edge, a plastic bag, gum, chewed, but still with a touch of peppermint, the black, gritty wheels of the cart.

Chapter 30: Please Don't Throw Food

Eleni Gabre-Madhin lived in Ethiopia until she was twelve, when she moved to the United States. Years later, during the famine in Ethiopia, she found herself at Cornell University when a food fight broke out in the cafeteria. She climbed onto the nearest table. "Stop doing this!" she said. "In my country people are starving."

At age forty-two, I knew she was the person I wanted to become, somebody who heard her own voice so loudly she would answer its call and climb onto a table without considering anyone else's reaction to her battle cry. I imagined myself on a table, my mouth open. "Please don't molest me," I would begin.

I've known only a few people who remind me of Eleni Gabre-Madhin. One of them is Walter Roberts, who began teaching eight years before I met him. When he arrived, some of his fourth graders were having trouble reading and doing simple math tasks. Many of them were from broken homes and neighborhoods that were falling apart. Mr. Roberts knew math and reading weren't foremost on his students' minds and began teaching them skills through discussions of real-life situations, making them write about their own lives and household struggles, the details of which were often heartbreaking. The students responded well, began to read better and to write journal entries with an honesty and rawness that often brought Mr. Roberts to tears. Mr. Roberts created an afterschool program to support their goals, and they named themselves the Roberts Scholars.

In the fall of 2006, I decided to teach a seminar comparing Italian and American education, which took place mostly within the walls of a classroom at my university. After the attack in 2007, though, I changed the class format completely. What started out as a careful examination of two cultures and their educational systems turned into a quest to understand our own system—what was working and what wasn't. One group of students suggested we visit the schools around us. I met Walter Roberts a few days later.

The day I visited his classroom for the first time, Mr. Roberts and I sat at a table across from each other and talked. He was one of the warmest people I had ever met. He asked me about my interest in education. I told him about my disappointment with No Child Left Behind and its focus on testing. "I was always thinking that now was not the time to act. But then my children and I were attacked and I realized life is short, things aren't always predictable, and I'd better get going. So here I am," I said. Mr. Roberts told me his story. "I had planned to go to graduate school after the first year of my teaching, but years later my scholars are thriving and I am still with them."

Mr. Roberts's students were from mostly low-income families. Many lived in apartment buildings near the school. His oldest students were just about to graduate from high school, and many of them returned to Mr. Roberts's class-room every Monday evening to participate in Roberts Scholars meetings. Every time I visited, the scholars' voices were strong. A student named Vincent spoke of another life, before Mr. Roberts's classroom. "I used to have a real bad attitude in first through fifth grade. Then sixth grade came around and Mr. Roberts said I was gifted in math. Until then I didn't know what my subject was. I changed my life around 'cause Mr. Roberts said that and now I want to be an engineer. It brought me eighty-eight thousand dollars in scholarships."

Colleen, president of the group, said, "I want to start an organization to help abused children because nobody helped me. It's going to be called 'Silent Screams.'"

There were times when his students weren't enthusiastic. "We're tired," they said one afternoon.

"Do you know you are tired because you don't sleep enough or eat well? It's important you guys eat healthily. There was a time when younger people had more energy than older people," Mr. Roberts said.

The day I brought my students to visit Mr. Roberts's fourth-grade classroom changed the way we talked about edu-cation in my class. My students were all freshmen. I was their first university teacher. Micaela had long, braided hair and a strong Jewish faith. She founded a mentoring partnership with our university and Mr. Roberts's students shortly after our visit. Ravi was from India. During high school he had felt a tremendous amount of pressure from his parents and often discussed this particular challenge with the class. Benjamin had curly, blond hair and looked like he could be my younger brother. Diya was an Indian American. She was passionate and stood her ground. Justine quietly changed the world, teaching sex education in Africa and joining Teach for America after college. Justine, Diya, and Micaela all became close friends.

There were also Deepika, Maneesha, Benjamin, Mia, and Anay, complex, motivated students who united around each other and the Roberts Scholars that year. Janine was my student assistant. She had taken my class a year before. With her encouragement, I looked up Mr. Roberts, and we took our first field trip to meet his students.

When we arrived, Mr. Roberts asked if we wanted to see the Line Game in action, an activity described in *The Freedom Writers Diary* by Erin Gruwell and her students. Mr. Roberts's students stood on either side of the room and he asked them questions. If they could answer yes to the question, they would move onto the line in the middle of the room.

"How many of you like ice cream?" he asked, and everyone stepped on the line.

"How many of you are angry that gas prices have gone up?"

Again, everyone stood on the line.

"Who did well on the last test?"

A handful of students stepped on the line.

"How many of you live in single-parent households?"

Most students moved to the center.

"Who has heard gunshots?" he said.

All of the scholars stood in the center.

"How many of you hear gunshots every night?"

Most students again returned to the center line.

My undergraduates didn't move. They stood quietly on the sidelines, mouths open.

On the way home, we all commented that we never hear gunshots in our neighborhoods. My most talkative student, Micaela, sat quietly, talking occasionally. "I'm impressed with how they can have such difficult experiences and still have so much hope," she said.

As Micaela said this, Justine and Diya sprang from their seats in the van. "We were just talking," Diya said. "We want to see the scholars again, and most of them have talked about going to college one day. Let's have a college day for them."

The day the fourth-grade Roberts Scholars arrived on campus, there were spurts of torrential downpour. My students took them on tours when the rain stopped. At lunch, while most of my students were in the cafeteria with the scholars, Ravi came into the classroom and sat with me. He began to talk about the scholars. "I can't believe it. In the class where I brought them, they were all taking notes and asking questions. I have been intimidated by the class size. I never speak up. I now realize how approachable my teacher is," Ravi said.

"You know," he said, "I grew up in a big house and I have never needed anything. But sometimes I don't work hard enough. The Roberts Scholars, they don't have much, but they do so much with what they have. They made me realize all I am capable of."

In the late afternoon, we brought in a college admissions counselor who asked the scholars questions and gave them advice about applying to colleges. At the end of the day, we lifted plastic cups of fizzy apple cider and toasted to our dreams.

One afternoon, four of my students accompanied me to visit the Roberts Scholars. Micaela asked if she could bring her grandparents.

When I arrived to pick them up, I could see Micaela's grandparents from the car window. They were well-dressed. Her grandfather wore a pressed blue suit and Micaela's grandmother had on a beautiful dark blue dress. I wondered if Mr. Roberts's students would feel on display with us there.

Micaela and her grandparents climbed into what my son liked to call "our old, rusty Volvo," and the other three students drove with Janine. All the way there I couldn't get my air conditioner to work. It was sweltering hot and we were caught in a traffic jam on a one-lane road that was under construction. We showed up at the Roberts Scholars classroom forty-five minutes late. Mr. Roberts welcomed us. He had been placing his students into learning-style groups and we walked in at the end of this process.

"Would the kinesthetic learners please stand," he said.

They did and the class went wild with applause.

"Would the visual learners rise?"

Again, applause and accolades.

After acknowledging each group, Mr. Roberts gave his students a math problem. As he made his way around the class, he asked his students about their learning styles and how to best address the problem. "Okay, my kinesthetic learners," he said, "what approach do you want to take on to solve this?"

We all joined the students and spoke with them about their learning styles, the math problems, their impressions of Mr. Roberts, their goals, and what it meant to be a scholar. They were happy to share, confident, open, eager, lovely. When I looked up again after a little less than an hour, I noticed Micaela's grandfather sitting in a chair wiping tears from his face with a handkerchief. I walked over to him.

"Are you okay?" I asked.

"This man," he said. "I can't believe what this man is doing."

Mr. Roberts asked some of his students to talk. They stood, telling us who they were, who they wanted to be one day, and how they were going to accomplish their goals. Then he asked us to speak. We all stood and told the scholars how much they had affected us. When Micaela's grandfather began to talk, the class went silent.

"I grew up poor," he said. "We had no money. I only stayed through eighth grade and then I had to quit school and work full time. We lived in the slums. The only reason I made it was because I used to sneak into the library and read. I read everything in that library. That's how I was educated. It saved me. What you children are doing. What you are doing, Mr. Roberts, I have never seen before. Please, you have so much to share with the world. You are such wonderful, beautiful, intelligent children. You are so smart. Please keep going in this direction and don't look back. You can do it. You can make a difference in this world. You can and you will and you are. You don't have to do it alone."

Micaela's grandfather was crying. I was, too. As I looked around the classroom, I realized everyone had tears in their eyes.

Then we left.

As Mr. Roberts gathered his students back into the classroom, we watched him from the open door.

"'Invictus' is a poem written from a hospital bed by William Ernest Henley, a victim of bone tuberculosis," he told them. Through determination and struggle, he lived thirty years longer than any doctor had predicted.

Mr. Roberts explained to his students that "Invictus" to him meant strength and courage in the face of adversity. That it meant hope when things seemed hopeless. "Anytime you feel there is no hope," he told his scholars, "recite 'Invictus' and you'll see the power you have inside of you."

Then a student who had memorized the poem recited it as though her life depended on it.

INVICTUS

OUT of the night that covers me,
Black as the Pit from pole to pole,
I thank whatever gods may be
For my unconquerable soul.

Christine Ristaino 143

In the fell clutch of circumstance
I have not winced nor cried aloud.
Under the bludgeonings of chance
My head is bloody, but unbowed.

Beyond this place of wrath and tears
Looms but the Horror of the shade,
And yet the menace of the years
Finds, and shall find, me unafraid.

It matters not how strait the gate,
How charged with punishments the scroll,
I am the master of my fate:
I am the captain of my soul.

On the day of the Roberts Scholars new member induction, Mr. Roberts asked me to talk about how the scholars had affected me and my students. It was an improvisational request, and I wondered how I could convey to parents just how much their children had given me. Then I remembered Eleni Gabre-Madhin standing on a table at Cornell University imploring her classmates not to throw food, and I knew what to say.

"Your children have pulled me from a rocky nightmare onto a warm, calm shore," I began, and then I told them about how the Roberts Scholars had made me feel part of the world again, how they had taken me and my students in, adopted us, and given us a home with them. I remembered a day when Mr. Roberts, his students, and I had lain on the floor of a classroom. We closed our eyes, and Mr. Roberts read a poem about his struggles with administrative policies, which had mandated he change his teaching methods. We all knew that Mr. Roberts would continue to reach his students despite these new policies.

"I'd like to thank somebody," Mr. Roberts had said. "I'd like to thank somebody for always believing in us, for inviting us to her school, for the sincerity, integrity, and love she has shared with us. Thank you, Dr. Ristaino."

I opened my eyes and looked at the ceiling, listened to the melodic, reassuring tones of Mr. Roberts's voice, and for a brief moment, I was one of them, part of the scholars' collective voice, part of the world's wholeness, part of Eleni Gabre-Madhin's message, sharing the human struggle as I lay on the floor in a classroom in Atlanta. Closing my eyes and stretching my body toward the infinite, I could have been anywhere and anyone in the world.

Retrogression 31:
September 15, 2007, 7:03 p.m.

The world around me has completely stopped. Nothing breathes. I lie on the ground, perfectly still, and then I take in a full breath.

Chapter 31: Juvie

Ada, Sam, and I are in the car and we have just passed that dreaded store. Snapshots of the attack flood into my mind, and I wonder if my children are having similar recollections. Ada begins telling me about her day. "In class we talked about how parents will always love you even when they're angry," she says. There is a pause. "Mom, I promise not to do this, but if I killed Sam, would you still love me?"

I look at my daughter in the rearview mirror. Despite what she just said, she seems angelic—blond, feathery hair, blue eyes, a whisper of a smile, and a face that is still cherublike at seven years old.

I look at Sam to see his reaction, but he's staring out the side window. My son's brown, button eyes shine. He is five years old and a boy's slender frame has finally taken over his chubby arms and legs.

"Ada, I love you," I say. "But I would be very angry at you for a long time. And, you know, I would lose two children. Sam would be dead and you would have to go to juvie."

Ada's eyes light up and Sam turns from the window. One of Ada's friends at school had told her about juvenile hall and ever since, juvie has been a topic of interest.

"Would you visit me?" Ada asks.

"Yes, after I calmed down," I respond.

"Mom?"

"Yes?"

"Can we change the subject?" Ada says.

"Sure," I say.

Nobody talks.

"Mom," Sam finally says. "Ada wouldn't be able to kill me because I would use my karate moves on her. Mom, did you know you should never get into a stranger's car even if he has a gun?"

"Yes, Sam. Probably he wouldn't use the gun unless you got into the car, right?"

"And the best place to kick someone is in the testicles," Sam says. "Or you can poke a person in the eyes."

"Sam, where did you learn this stuff?" I ask.

"Karate," he tells me.

"Mom," Ada says. "I really want to poke somebody's eyes out. I hope I get to one day."

"I don't," I say. "It would mean you were in real danger."

"But you don't know how angry I am. I could really do it. I want to, Mom."

"Tell me, sweetie, what are you angry about?" I ask.

"I'm angry at that man. I'm angry because when he was hurting you I didn't do anything," she says.

"But, Ada, none of us knew what to do."

"But I could have poked his eyes out. He was hurting you and I just watched."

My daughter begins to cry and in the rearview mirror I see Samuel practicing his karate moves on her leg.

"Sam!" I warn as I reach my arm back and grab one of Ada's hands.

"You were there for me. You and Sam hugged me. You made me feel loved and protected. Now Samuel's learning karate and you and I do aikido. If this ever happens again, we'll be ready."

When we arrive home, I tell Mark about our conversation. Later I find him and Ada talking in her room, Mark's legs stretched lengthwise on the bed, his feet hanging over the edge. I can see Ada's blond hair and my husband's bald head on the pillow.

"I felt helpless, too," he says. "I wish so much I could have been there to protect you, but I wasn't with you. Over and over again I ask myself, 'Why wasn't I there?' But I wasn't and I have to accept that."

I don't enter the room. It's dusk and I need to make lunches. There's school tomorrow.

Retrogression 32:
September 15, 2007, 7:02 p.m.

A hand shoots toward my eye, blackness, agonizing, spots of light, the way I imagine cartoon stars to be. I jerk, let go of the cart, and fall. The back of my head hits the ground.

Chapter 32: Relocated Yankees

My aunt and uncle moved from Massachusetts to Augusta, Georgia, in the late fifties, and as a child I heard stories about their trip. It seemed a foreign land and a different time. They described their experiences in the South—different water fountains, bathrooms, and rules for African Americans and whites.

"Things were so bad there," my uncle Art once said, "that President Eisenhower had to come down South and personally try to set things right."

Aunt Mary talked about her experience in 1956 working at a hospital where correspondence from local white farmers to other whites was often written at a fourth-grade level.

Aunt Mary's closest friend from Augusta was well-mannered and kind to my aunt. At the end of their stay in Georgia, Aunt Mary waited for an elevator with her friend on a spring day. When a black man walked in front of her friend and got into the elevator first, this dignified, polite woman used words Aunt Mary doesn't care to repeat.

"She was a cute girl," my aunt said, "and did she have manners. I loved her. Then, one day I was waiting for an elevator and this happened. I wondered, 'Who is this woman and where did my sweet friend go?' In the South I never felt completely at home, all these rules I didn't understand, and the southerners liked and hated us northerners at the same time. They often said to your uncle and me, of course with a smile on their faces, 'You Yankees are like hemorrhoids. You come down here. You won't go back up. And you're all a pain in the ass.'"

Years later, I, too, made my trek to the South to take up residence, as Aunt Mary and Uncle Art had, but in different times. In Atlanta, because I worked at a university that was exploring its past, I often had the opportunity to talk about the unfavorable conditions of the South, the segregation my aunt and uncle had witnessed firsthand. One discussion occurred a few years after my attack, when I was participating in the Transform Faculty Seminar. The seminar was set up to give faculty the tools to discuss and explore race at a university setting. The main focus of the workshop was the university's history with race. The university was originally located forty miles away in a small town in Georgia, and on the third day of the workshop, we boarded a bus and went there.

My favorite part of this visit involved a conversation with T.J. Mannor, Jr., who arrived unceremoniously into this world in 1936. T.J.'s grandfather was born around 1837 in Alabama. According to T.J., his grandfather and his grandfather's brother were brought to campus as enslaved children. As an adult, his grandfather was a rock mason and his grandfather's brother, a brick mason. Both brothers provided free labor to help build the town, which included an old church, now a historical treasure.

We heard from anthropologist Joseph Land, who had explored the town's history with his students through various partnerships with the community. He spoke of how when his class began to interview local citizens, they were reticent to speak. Nevertheless, because of their work together, the two communities became more and more comfortable with each other.

One project stands out for me. A segregated cemetery has existed in this town for over a century. The white section of the city cemetery has always been maintained and manicured, but the African American portion was once overgrown with weeds and underbrush. There had also been a clear cut by a pulpwood merchant around 1990 that only affected the black section of the cemetery, damaging many of the headstones. The students learned of this problem from the local black community, and in collaboration with its members, began working at the cemetery to unearth the gravestones and beautify the land. The most surprising gardener was a Vietnam veteran, somewhat of a loner, who, after learning about the project, became an avid participant. Through his work with students and local African Americans, he found his way back into the community. When he developed pancreatic cancer a year into the project, it was the black community and a handful of students who spent his final days with him.

At around the same time as the cemetery project, students also created an oral history of the town's black inhabitants. Joseph Land told us about Cecelia Smith, who felt extremely uncomfortable revealing personal details about her experiences as a black woman. But one day she did open up, quite surprisingly, during the most mundane of demonstrations.

The students were at her house. Ms. Smith showed them how at nine years old she had ironed the clothes of white men and women from the area. "Back and forth, back and forth," Joseph remembered her saying. And then she said something they almost didn't catch. "When you ironed a white garment and there was a crease that just wouldn't iron down, that's how you knew."

One of Joseph's students blanched.

Another student asked, "Knew what?"

"Think about it," she told them. "When you ironed and ironed, but you couldn't iron away a crease."

They imagined Klansmen, burning crosses, and white, pointy hoods, the type of point impossible to iron away.

"You think of the Klan as a secret society, but they had servants and they had to get their clothes cleaned, too. And who do you think did these things for them?" Joseph asked us. "So there were moments like that when my students were stunned at what they learned."

In the afternoon, we had a chance to talk with Margaret Ashton, an associate professor of history. Margaret spoke about two historical figures at the university, Atticus Greene Haygood, who was elected president of the Board of Trustees in 1875, and Andrew Sledd, a turn-of-the-century professor. Both men were controversial figures. Sledd wrote an essay for the *Atlantic Monthly* denouncing lynching. Haygood supported full citizenship of former slaves and the idea of harmony between the races. However, both men, when writing about their ideas, which were quite progressive for the time, peppered their thoughts with the common beliefs held in the Old South, such as the idea that blacks belonged to an inferior race.

At a certain point I commented, "When I read these two men, I wonder what they really thought. I wonder if they had to work within the codes of the time in order to obtain a certain readership, to protect themselves and their jobs, or to get people to listen to them. Maybe little by little they had hoped to change people."

Margaret looked at me and paused. I could tell she was struggling to find the right words. "I can't go there," she finally said. "I don't feel like making assumptions that aren't on the page. Yes, they were progressive, but there are things I can't really forget."

Margaret's comments sobered me. There were so many issues I had glossed over during my lifetime, so many things I had wanted to forget.

At the end of our visit, we were asked to create a list of assumptions we had held before the workshop, ideas we wished to let go of, bury. Optimism, I wrote. It had always been my coping mechanism. But how could racism, violence, rape, abuse, any of this, be viewed through an optimistic lens? Perhaps I could still be optimistic about the future, while keeping a more realistic understanding of the past. I would try. I buried my old approach to life under a tree with the others and boarded the bus.

Retrogression 33:

September 15, 2007,

7:01 p.m. and 43 seconds

The man has my purse in both hands and tugs harder at it now. We lock eyes. "You're a prick," I say.

Chapter 33:
Missed Opportunities

"**E**very child should take Omega 3," our pediatrician had said to my husband and me; so I was in the health food store during a cold rainstorm buying fish oil for an astronomical price.

The health food store had a spicy warmth about it that enraptured me. *I could stay here all day looking at the wonder products and how they would improve my life*, I thought. I walked by a woman with braided black hair, light brown skin, and a bright yellow dress that illuminated her face. I smiled at her. "How are you?" I said.

"What do you care how I am?" she asked as she picked up a product off the shelf and put it into her basket. "Sometimes people say things they don't mean."

I can't tell you her words didn't sting or that after she walked away, I didn't cry. I did; but I managed to say before skulking off to a less-trafficked area of the store, "How do you know I didn't mean it? I really did."

I had meant it. I wanted her smile to lift me up as her brightly colored clothes had. That deep yellow had beckoned me to make a connection, to comment on the crappy, rainy day we were having and how the warmth of the health food store and spicy smells enveloped us, made us smile at strangers and ask them how they were.

Shortly after the attack, I was driving my son home from school and we were stopped at a red light. My son wanted Cheerios so I reached back to hand him some. The next thing I knew, I had tapped the car in front of us with my bumper. A black man jumped out of his car before I even registered what had happened. I opened my door.

"I'm sorry," I said to him. "I was giving my son Cheerios and my foot must have let up on the brake."

The man didn't say a word, just stared at me as though I had killed his best friend. He inspected his vehicle, looked at me again, and then walked slowly to his car door. I wanted to ask him if he was angry about the bumper or something much less obvious. By now the red light had changed to green and he drove away.

A colleague sued my department because she hadn't been compensated well for a project. When Arlene did this, I couldn't believe she would ask for so much money when nobody else involved in the project had been paid a cent. Academics research for the love of their work, right?

"Is this how the daughter of a man who went to jail for his beliefs behaves? Would your father be proud of you now?" she had asked when I failed to understand her rationale.

Eleven months later another colleague accused two policemen of racial profiling when they pulled him over on his bicycle for not having a taillight. Years before, he had been blindsided by the gun of an undercover cop, who thought he was stealing his father's car, and also arrested for no good reason while walking to a bus stop. These two events set him up to be wary of the police, to protest for civil rights, and to recognize racial profiling almost before it happens. Talking with this friend helped me understand both his and Arlene's actions. Despite the many risks they took, both colleagues were hoping to change a system that wasn't fair to begin with.

One weekend toward the end of spring, the children, Mark, and I went to Fort Mountain in North Georgia with twelve Unitarian Universalist families. It was a beautiful day and as we descended a tree-covered hill, we spotted a lake with a beach in front of us.

My children were fully clothed—pants, shoes, socks, underwear, long-sleeved shirts. They began to take off their shoes and socks before we even arrived at the beach, and within moments, my children, clothes and all, were in the water, pushing off the sandy floor with their toes, gliding into the cold lake, coming up for air, floating, wiggling, touching hands for a moment, opening their mouths, laughing, exploring every inch of the bottom. Most of the other children stood looking at mine and then at their parents for permission to join them, but my children hadn't asked. I stood watching them, proud of their recklessness, amazed by their desire to experience everything so completely. I wanted to join them, fully clothed, but stood on the sidelines with the others.

I have spent years admiring my brothers from a distance. They are artists, writers, actors. They are kind, humble, outgoing, shy. What always strikes me when I see them is how they know exactly who they are. Their voices seem to inhabit their bodies and their true selves spill out into everything they do. I long to ask them how this is possible, how they do it, but usually, in their presence I feel like their groupie, a teenager standing quietly next to the boy band she loves. I try to decide if this tongue-tiedness is a missed opportunity, a failure to communicate with them fully, or if this state is simply the result of the opportunity I had to grow up with people I admire. When I think about my childhood, if I go back far enough, I realize they don't entirely know me. I've never been completely honest with them about my experiences.

My niece Charlotte lives who she is. She expresses herself beautifully—in person, on canvas, through narrative. When reading her stories, I realize Charlotte and I are both grappling with how to best be ourselves, only from different stages of our lives, for I am a forty-two-year-old woman and she is fifteen.

Charlotte's parents, Cooper and Olivia, are both from New Zealand, and they are grounded, attractive, real. Cooper is a pathologist and after spending the day with dead people, likes to come home, have a glass of wine, and talk about books, music, art, photography. He is a fabulous photographer. One of his best photos is of Charlotte wearing a tribal mask swinging on a tire from a tall tree in their backyard.

Olivia has a business called "Bold Girls" and Charlotte used to model sleek, sparkly girl-power skirts, capes, and crowns for Olivia's website until she became a teenager. The message behind Olivia's designs: dress up as your boldest, most wonderful self, not as somebody else. Olivia stands under a Bold

Girl sign on her website, in red, red lipstick, large earrings, and a black shirt with red trim. "Every Girl is a Bold Girl!" she says. Olivia tells us how observing a three-year-old Charlotte, a girl who swung to the highest reaches of the earth on her wooden swing, who dressed up in skirts and capes and became anyone she wanted, and whose books brought her to faraway places every day, inspired her to start a business. Even at three, Charlotte knew who she was, infinitely aware of possibility.

Charlotte is a fencer and her coach is an Olympic coach, the type you always hear about—strict, personable, explosive, demanding. He loves Charlotte and is grooming her for the 2012 Olympic games.

The day I finally went to a fencing match, I had been babysitting a friend's son for the weekend. He was at my house when I left, but I went anyway since every time Charlotte mentioned her competitions there was always some kind of conflict—a birthday party, a work obligation, dishwasher repairman, exhaustion—two years of missed opportunities. I felt credibility slipping each time I told her I really did want to go.

"Shit," I said when I realized there was yet another conflict.

"It's fine," my husband told me. "I'm okay with the kids."

So on the day of the match, I left my house, climbed into my car, and drove the twenty miles or so to her gym.

It was a quiet Sunday afternoon. The highways were still dark from a fresh rain. I could see trees on the side of the road and the rain made me believe the air in Atlanta was fresh and clean, as though I should take in large, full breaths.

As I entered the gym, I felt an energy not much different from that of high school swim meets long ago. I didn't see Charlotte when I first arrived, just lots of high school girls and boys in slick, blue fencing uniforms. They talked, laughed, and ate bagels from a table in the center of the foyer. I walked past a long stretch of offices and moved into a clearing filled with mats and fencers. My brother-in-law was on a mat in front of me, keeping score for a match between two older boys. He nodded at me and continued his work. Charlotte was over to the side, involved in a conversation with two teenage girls. She was beautiful—tall with long, blond hair, clear skin, and animated blue eyes. She stood gracefully, falling easily into conversation. I could see her smile, gesture, lean intently to listen, think for a moment, respond.

I looked up at the warehouse ceiling and spotted old banners announcing the Olympic debut of two girls from the gym. I had watched them on television as they stood on the podium wearing third-place team medals. Charlotte was almost as good as they were, I remembered Cooper telling me. I thought of Charlotte leaving us, heading to a foreign country in less than four years to fence as an Olympic athlete, and tears filled my eyes. This place was part of Charlotte, a place that, until today, I had never experienced with her. I wiped my tears and fresh ones replaced them. Then I wiped those away, too.

I sat alone on bleachers and took in the action around me. When we first moved to Atlanta, my husband and I had spent afternoons with Charlotte in the city center eating ice-cream cones, at Six Flags amusement parks, at bookstores. But after my children were born, we stopped bringing Charlotte out. I missed these afternoons with her.

Charlotte looked up, saw me, began to walk in my direction, and I put my hand on her arm when she arrived. *I will come to all her competitions from now on*, I thought. But then I remembered, life has a way of changing things just when we feel we're in control, and I revised my plan—well maybe some of them. I hugged Charlotte and then Cooper was standing next to us, too, and there was a man with a Ukrainian accent, white hair, self-assured, wearing a blue Olympic jacket over a white shirt, walking in our direction, his hand outstretched.

During my leave of absence, my colleague Antonia and I met on a Saturday to talk about my future with our project. We walked and the air felt heavy. My steps were heavy.

"I can tell your heart is no longer in this project," she said.

Antonia was referring to an online teaching method she created and we had codified in two textbooks and countless articles. It was a huge endeavor, one I had been working on with Antonia since my son was two months old. While he slept, strapped to my chest, I typed. There was an energy about this work—a feeling we could make changes in our field, become better teachers—but since the attack, I had been a lame duck, no longer willing to put in the long hours necessary to make the project a success, feeling the tug of my children and husband post-trauma, and a need to write.

"It has been great," I said. "I have learned so much. But no. You are right. I want to focus on my family."

"The door will always be open for you if you decide to come back," she told me.

But I knew I would never go back to this project, even though I was closing the door on something I enjoyed and believed in. In front of me for miles, I could see a trajectory of missed opportunities—conferences never attended, people never met, topics not discussed, unrealized articles, conversations with my colleague about teaching perhaps never fulfilled. And then, barely visible, something I had not noticed in a long time, perhaps never noticed before, another path, my own, about to be claimed.

Retrogression 34:
September 15, 2007,
7:01 p.m. and 30 seconds.

I am stunned and in pain. My jaw is aching and I look at the
man in front of us for some kind of explanation.

Chapter 34:
Nolo Contendere

"If somebody had come to my house and asked me for an ID, I would have been pissed off," my father says. "And I would have told him, too."

We are having dinner at my parents' place in Maine and talking about Harvard scholar Henry Gates, a black man who was arrested in Cambridge, Massachusetts by a white officer for trespassing on his own property.

"His big mistake was following the cop out and arguing with him," my husband replies.

"He was pissed," my father says. "I would have done the same thing."

"Look, Bernie. If you and I were having an argument—"

My father interrupts. "Like we are now."

"Yes. If we were arguing like we are now, and I walked away from the argument to collect myself and you followed and kept yelling at me, I would probably have turned around and clocked you one," Mark says.

"You would have clocked a seventy-year-old man?" my father asks and smiles.

"Yeah," Mark says, laughing.

"Well, you bastard," my father says and then all of us are laughing.

"This officer," I say, "he teaches a class to police on how to avoid racial profiling, so maybe his actions weren't racially motivated."

"But Gates is one of the most respected men in his field," my father says. "I'm sure he was really upset. He's worked hard to get where he is. One of the top guys in his field, and then this man is at his door asking him for an ID."

"The man was only doing what he was supposed to do," my brother Zach says. "Somebody called the police. He was obligated to go there."

"Yes, but he could have done it differently. He could have talked it out with this man. He didn't have to come on so strong."

Mark looks at my father. "Gates probably totally pissed off the cop with his attitude. He was screaming and swearing at him. There's a photo of him taken by a man who happened to be passing by, and you can see Gates in handcuffs and his mouth is all twisted as though he's still yelling. But when you're with a cop, you can't swear and yell at him like that."

"Yeah, but that's no reason to arrest him. What about freedom of speech?" my father says. "And again, he's worked hard to get to where he is. You and Christine know how tough graduate school and academia are. Doesn't he have a right to claim his successes? Shouldn't he be pissed off beyond belief when this guy tries to arrest him?"

I think about Gates's position at Harvard. He went all the way in academia, a top researcher in his field. And yet yelling at authority figures is something I've never had the courage to do in my life. I've always been polite. "But Dad," I say. "Isn't there some law that says we can't yell at the police?"

"How can there be? Freedom of speech. The police are tougher than that. They can take a bit of yelling."

"But that's not the point, Dad," I say. "If a student in junior high used the F-word. If he said, 'Mr. Ristaino, fuck you,' you would have sent that student to the principal's office and he would have been suspended."

"Yes, so what?"

"Well," Mark says, "jail is the police version of suspension."

"No, it's not. They had no right to drag this man to jail because he was swearing at the police. Plus they dropped the charges, which means he wasn't guilty."

"Of course they dropped the charges," Mark says. "Of course he's not guilty. It's his house—he wasn't breaking in."

"But if they were white guys trying to get into Gates's apartment, I'm sure the neighbor wouldn't have called the police," Zach says. "I think that's why Obama said what he did when he initially heard the story. Because there's such a history here when it comes to calling the police on black men."

"This is the first time Obama has come out strongly on a race issue," Mark comments. "Every black man has to deal with racial profiling. The problem is though, as soon as Obama put in his first unscripted words on the matter, true as they are, the press went crazy, saying he was taking sides."

"Obama's calling both men over to the White House to have beer and pretzels so they can patch things up," I say.

"It's really just a photo op," Mark says. "On the other side of the coin, it's true that white people are afraid of black men who commit crimes. Christine, sorry for going against the premise of your book, but I think all of you here have either been attacked or mugged by black men, and anyone who has been in that type of situation has some hurdles to jump over afterward."

Ernie admits, "The guys who held me up were black. Zach, all of those times you were mugged, were you mugged by black men?"

"Yes," Zach states.

"I wasn't robbed by a black man. He was white," my brother George says with a Boston accent. "That night I was robbed at the sub shop, the guy didn't know I was there. There were two girls working, and I was bending over, getting some meat out of the refrigerator. He didn't see me, just these two women. They're from Woonsocket so, you know, I thought he was one of their asshole friends." George laughs. "He's this white guy, and I don't realize he has a gun even though he's already told them. I can see they're totally freaking out, so I stand, and that guy turns even whiter when he realizes I'm there. And I go, 'What does he want?' And then he says, 'I got a gun, and I want your money.'"

George pauses, almost for dramatic effect.

"That's the second time he's said it, but the first time I've heard him. I can feel the exact spot in my brain where the adrenalin bursts out into my body, the exact spot, and now I'm hearing everything he's saying. I have about two hundred dollars of tips in my pocket, and my wallet with about fifty bucks in that, but I don't tell him. I just start emptying out the cash register and then I lift up the drawer and say, 'Hey, sometimes we have twenties down here.' We didn't give him much, and when the cops came, we couldn't agree on what he looked like—was he white or Mexican."

My father laughs.

George continues, "The two girls were arguing like crazy. But I remember his face, every inch of it. He was white."

My father sighs. "In this country we are insane, insane people allowed to carry guns. This week the Senate just barely got this thing taken out of a bill that would have let people take weapons into a state that didn't allow weapons—as long as they had a permit from the place where they bought it. This would mean that in Massachusetts, which doesn't allow anyone to have guns, people could bring their guns here if they had a permit from somewhere else. So I learned this bill didn't pass, but upon looking into it further, I realized fifty senators, that's half of them, voted in favor of it, which means a number of Democrats were so scared to go against it that they voted for it. Why the hell, in a country that supposedly has smart people in it, would we want guns around?"

"Well, isn't it from the founding fathers—the right to protect ourselves?" my mother asks.

"You're absolutely right, Sandra. That's why. But people have really gone crazy with this right. They think they can carry semiautomatic weapons. It's as though they think it says, 'you have the right to bear Uzis' rather than arms. And who really needs a gun anyway?"

I'm back in Georgia, on my way to court. I have decided to fight a traffic ticket even though it's obvious I have broken the law, gone nineteen miles over the speed limit. I listen as the judge calls people up one by one. There are two stop sign violations and the judge drops the fine by one hundred dollars each. Then there's a man who has brought in tons of evidence. First the police officer stands. He tells the judge he has had extensive training in estimating speed limits, that this is the way police used to ticket people in the past based on training, their eyes, a siren, and a citation. He is very good at this and although he did not have a laser to track the exact speed, he believes the offender was going twenty miles over the speed limit.

The man speaks next. He immediately states that the officer has misrepresented his case. "The officer said I was late for a golf game. I was not. I was on my way to the golf course and I told him to hurry up because I would be late for the tee. As you can see by this piece of paper, I was not late because it began at 7:30 a.m., and it was 7:15 a.m. when I was pulled over."

The man goes on to show the officer and the judge a map of the golf course and the street where he was pulled over and questions if the officer could see him driving at all from his vantage point.

"I'm going to knock off a hundred and fifty dollars," the judge says. "Because you prepared well, had a lot of information, and brought up some good points. However, please don't tell an officer to hurry up. He's just doing his job. It would be like telling me to hurry up. If I want to do a good job, I need a certain amount of time to do so. It's disrespectful. I didn't hold that against you when I made this decision. You prepared well. But you need to understand."

Then it's my turn. I explain my situation. "I'm hoping you can be lenient with this ticket," I say to the judge. "The reason I was going faster than normal was because I was in my husband's car. My car's transmission had been failing for months, and it took all kinds of effort to get it going every time I got to a stop sign or turned a corner. My husband had taken my car to be fixed, and he commented later that my car barely drove for him. So I think I was pushing hard on the gas in my husband's car to make it go. But it went just fine . . . too fine, in fact."

"Unfortunately, ma'am, this would have been a good time to have chosen 'nolo contendere.' This is an unfortunate case because 'nolo contendere' was made for people like you who don't have a record."

"Can I claim it now?" I ask.

"No, you've already contended it with me. I'm sorry, ma'am, but I'm going to have to say you're guilty. Your speed was clocked on the radar."

The day of the ticket I had driven thirty-five miles to pick up a used bike for Samuel. It was his birthday, and we couldn't afford to buy a new one. But the used bike with a price tag of twenty-five dollars would now cost us close to $300 after I paid the ticket.

"But nobody told me 'nolo contendere' was even an option," I argue.

"There were plenty of opportunities to talk with the counsel."

"Yes, I went to the counsel. She asked me, 'So you want to say not guilty?' I said 'yes' and she told me to sit down. Although I had heard of 'nolo contendere' before, I had been confused about its function. And she didn't mention this option at all."

"Sorry, ma'am. There's nothing I can do now."

I turn to the officer, whose eyes show compassion for my situation. They had been the same way the day he gave me the ticket. "Why don't you come to the court date," he had told me. "If you don't have a record, they'll be lenient." Had I understood the system, I could have spared myself the extra points.

I realize court has gone horribly wrong, but I'm not unhappy that I'm standing in front of the judge, not having done my homework. It has taught me something. I shake the officer's hand and then I look back at the judge before I pick up my things and leave. The judge had made it clear to the golf course man there is a code of conduct he should have followed when talking with the police. But my minor run-in with the law has made me a bit edgy and unsatisfied, and Gates had a lot more at stake than I did. Perhaps I understand why Gates had to do what he did, why he needed to challenge an authority figure when he thought he was being served an injustice, that his life, his voice, his whole being depended on it; or why my father, years before, had served ten days in jail to change an unfair maternity policy in his school system; and why the golf course man had brought in evidence to refute an officer who had eyeballed his speed. Nothing I say to the judge this day is profound, but at least I speak up, proclaim that I feel my circumstances are unfair in a system where the only people who understand the language are repeat offenders. "I wish somebody had explained things to me a bit better," I say.

It has taken me years to get here, years to be able to comment on my own rights to this judge, years to even realize I have rights to begin with. I wonder, had I told my parents immediately about the man, would I have lived my whole life differently?

Retrogression 35:
September 15, 2007,
7:01 p.m. and 25 seconds.

A shooting pain rips through my jaw. My head jerks backward. My neck twists. I curl my fingers tighter around the bar of the cart and grip it with everything I have.

Chapter 35:
Gidget's Got Gadgets

We have adopted a dog named Gidget. She has a bung ear that flops over while the other one stands straight up. When I saw little Gidget with that flopped over ear, I knew she should be part of our family.

Whenever there's a thunderstorm, Gidget begins to shake like she's having a mini-convulsion. The first time she did it, we brought her to the vet. "Lots of dogs shake when it thunders outside," the vet told us. "It's nothing. She's fine."

Every day when we leave the house, Gidget moans and barks and puts on a good show, begging to join us. We always feel terrible. But one day Sam says with a serious face, "It's a cover."

"How do you mean?" I ask.

"She's pretending to be upset, but as soon as we leave, all the dogs from the neighborhood come over through these invisible secret agent tubes that are attached to our house. They're doing it now."

"Yeah," Ada chimes in. "She just doesn't want us to suspect anything."

"Well, how do you know about the tubes?" I ask.

"I think I saw one coming out of the ceiling she forgot to close," Sam says.

"Gidgie uses a special gadget," Ada says.

Sam begins to sing, as if on cue, "Gidget's got gadgets." Ada and I pick up the tune and join in. We repeat the refrain over and over again, then Sam sings at the top of his lungs, "The pet store is really an agency." Ada and I repeat, "Gidget's got gadgets, Gidget's got gadgets" and then we all sing loudly the pet store line, perfect harmony.

Retrogression 36:

September 15, 2007, 7:01 p.m.

I hold on to the cart tightly, as though it could stabilize me, save me, protect my children, change things.

Chapter 36:
Preaching to the Choir

My children join the Sharks swim team near our home. Samuel has just mastered the crawl; Ada is racing freestyle and backstroke and winning second- and third-place ribbons. I'm so proud of them. At the pool there's a woman named Lily who has tons of energy and unofficially runs the swim meets. Somehow she manages to organize hundreds of parents and children and make everything go smoothly. I am always in awe. She is short and vocal and wears a shark fin on her head. During practice, she often tells late swimmers to arrive on time. "My daughters look up to you," she says to them. "Don't let them down."

Lily and I talk about her job, her partner and their two daughters, religion, and the Obama administration as our children enjoy themselves in the pool. At a certain point in our conversation, my son runs by. I touch his head. "Hey, my little flower," I say and smile.

When Sam was a baby, his eyes were so shiny and animated they seemed to pop out of his face. My husband called him button eyes, but for me his eyes held joy and beauty and I called him flower.

When Samuel hit preschool, this name continued to represent my son for me, but when I said it, often parents would frown. "You've got to stop calling him that," they would say. "He'll get a lot of grief one day for that name." I would try to explain why Sam to me was a flower, but most of my comments fell on deaf ears.

When Lily hears me call Samuel a flower, she kneels close to him and says, "Did I just hear your mom call you a flower?"

"I know, I know," I say. "Kids will make fun of him. I can't help it, though. He's a flower to me."

Lily's posture changes and she stands. "If you are going to worry about what other people think, then you better leave this pool right now," she states and I can tell she means it.

Lily begins to walk away from me but I follow.

"Thank you for saying that," I say, realizing I've done exactly what I battle against most of the time.

"Don't do this to your kids!" Lily tells me. "Be strong for them. Don't buy into that. Flowers can be male. Just because you call him flower doesn't mean he's going to be gay."

"But it's more than fine if he's gay," I say. "I want him to be who he is."

But Lily shakes her head. For her perhaps I have become somebody who doesn't respect her, who doesn't understand her struggle. There is a part of me that knows she has misunderstood me completely. I get her. But part of me knows I need to hear what Lily has to say. I think of Lily, a lesbian woman from the South who has probably fought her entire life for her sexual identity. Would she really have condemned me because my son's essence reminded me of flowers?

Lily leaves with her girls a few minutes later. It's lunch time. The kids and I gather our things and leave, too. In the past I would have agonized over this conversation, but this time I'm sure it will be okay. It's still a good day.

Retrogression 37:
September 15, 2007, 7:00 p.m.

My purse strap tears at my arm and cuts into it. I try to adjust the strap by lifting my shoulder and thrusting it backward, but the strap resists and continues to pull.

Chapter 37: Raising Men

A little girl bent over to pick something up and my son kissed her on the butt. I was glad I was on the phone with his teacher when she told me because it was hard to keep a straight face, even though I wasn't particularly happy with the news.

"Samuel, why did you do that?" Mark asks him at dinner.

"Her bum was right in front of me, so I kissed it," he says.

"Yes, but it's not a good idea to do that. You never kiss girls on the bum. And you don't kiss people unless they say it's okay."

"Okay, Dad," Samuel says. "I won't do it anymore."

Later that evening, Samuel is chasing Ada around the house.

"Mom, Sam is trying to kiss my butt," Ada says.

"Samuel," I say. "What were we telling you earlier? You cannot touch or kiss people on the rear end. It's not allowed," I tell him.

A few minutes later I feel something jabbing through the side of my jeans and turn to see Samuel with a pencil, giggling.

"Did you just poke me?" I ask.

He runs off.

"Don't poke people," I yell.

Then I hear Ada's voice. "Sam, cut it out!"

I run into Ada's room and take away the pencil. I grab Sam's arms, one in each hand.

"Samuel, did you just poke Ada even though I asked you not to?"

"Yes," he says.

"Samuel, this is serious." I tighten my grip. "When a girl says no, what do you do?" I ask.

"You stop," he says and looks away from me.

"That's right." I lift his chin and steer it toward my face. "When a girl says no, what do you do?"

"You stop," he says.

"Yes. When a girl says no, what do you do?"

"You stop," he answers.

"Yes. That's right. When a girl says no, what do you do?"

"You stop."

"Yes, you stop. You stop. You stop. Please, if you remember anything, remember that. If a girl says no, what do you do?"

Retrogression 38:

September 15, 2007,

6:59 p.m. and 35 seconds.

He lifts his free hand, a train pummeling toward sheet rock. Crack. Something hits my nose. I am drowning in red, blood pouring out of my nostrils. Somebody gasps, whimpers, maybe my daughter.

Chapter 38: Waiting Women of the Eighties

A friend from college calls me. Natalie is on her way to meet her biological mother. She tells me about her plans as she drives on Highway 95 toward Virginia. She can't believe she's doing this. I had always known I'd be getting this phone call, that Natalie's desire to find out who she was would lead her here.

Today we speak about how adoption has shaped her. "I had a conversation with Simon the other day about going to visit my birth mother. He was supportive and cared. Something seemed to melt right there inside me. I was his niece and he was my uncle, not his adopted niece, just his niece," she says.

"I think that's how he's always viewed you," I say.

"I know. I know. But I've always felt adopted. Maybe it's something I imposed on myself, but I never felt I was the real thing. I never looked like anyone in my family. I thought perhaps they viewed me as different, too."

"Have you told the kids?" I ask.

"Not yet," Natalie says. "I want to establish something with her first so I can define it for them. So they'll be open to it and won't feel threatened."

"Yes, that makes sense."

"Because this year has been difficult for them. They've had to redefine so many relationships."

I nod into the phone.

Natalie surprised everyone two years ago when she told us she was an alcoholic. Nobody believed her. But she had been drinking for years to cope with her husband's alcoholism. She went to AA and asked her husband to join her. He didn't.

"It's hard to live with an alcoholic once you've quit," she told me. "He made a choice—not to join me. So we're moving in separate directions."

Natalie and I begin talking about our family histories with alcoholism. Both of us had grandparents who were alcoholics, and Natalie's mother-in-law was an alcoholic, too.

"Mark recently read an article written by the child of an alcoholic," I tell Natalie. "The interesting thing is that after he read it he said, 'I know you're not the daughter of an alcoholic, Christine, but you sure do share some of the same characteristics with this guy.' Our mothers have modeled for us all their coping mechanisms," I say. "We've watched them and learned how daughters of alcoholics interact with the world."

"I know," she replies. "So I don't know if my worries in college were based on these things I learned from my mother or because I was adopted."

Natalie and I enjoyed college a little too much our first couple of years. We met through my roommate Jo. Some of my favorite memories are with these two women—Jo and Natalie often invited me to bonfires in the woods with a group of friends who religiously followed the Grateful Dead. I enjoyed many evenings in conversation with half my body cold and the other half warmed by the fire with background music, all of us under a veil of stars. Once we spent hours riding the elevator in a towerlike dorm, listening to a musician Jo had a crush on as he played his guitar and sang in the middle of the elevator. Each time the door opened, we'd laugh with the unsuspecting visitors. Then the doors would close again and they would leave our world. Jo and I played backgammon as a drinking game, complained about two old boyfriends who had broken our hearts, and played practical jokes on our suitemates in the early morning hours. With Natalie we took trips into the mountains and drank beer at high altitudes, camped a half hour away, doing homework by flashlight.

"I did silly things in college," I admit to Natalie.

"I did silly things, too," she says. "Most of the time you were with me. But part of the reason we did these things was because the eighties were a terrible time for women. Women weren't sure where they belonged. And people didn't talk back then. Women were left flailing, so we just had fun instead. Today there's so much momentum and people telling young women they can do it."

"I like what we're telling our daughters these days," I say to Natalie. "Please call me after you talk with your birth mother."

As I hang up the phone, I realize we've all become who we were supposed to be, but perhaps not in the form our college selves would have recognized. Natalie is a single mother of two, a niece, a teacher, a reformed alcoholic with a mature sense of self. Jo is an oceanographer in Seattle, a lifeline for a friend with Lou Gehrig's Disease, an animal lover. I am a teacher, a mother of two, a wife, and now, a writer. The events of our past, even the elevator ride, have led us to this place.

Retrogression 39:
September 15, 2007,
6:59 p.m. and 33 seconds.

The man places a hand on the handle of the cart. He's facing the wrong way and putting even more weight on the cart instead of lifting it. I want to tell him, but maybe he has a different plan, and my purse seems to be caught on something.

Chapter 39:
Going Soft

Over and over again people take advantage of Ada, something I often experienced too as a child. Ada becomes outraged when this happens. She can't believe people do this.

One day I overhear the kids talking in the backseat of the car on the way home from school.

"Everyone got one on a cupcake. Mine had a lighted circle on it, and you could see this red prick of light on the ceiling as it shined all the way up there. I wanted to give it to you, Sam, because I knew you would like it. But Francis wanted mine and he didn't have one, so I gave it to him."

"Ada," Sam says, "you have to say no once and they'll stop asking."

"Sam, I can't help myself. I don't want to go hard or anything."

"Ada, you can say no. Feel free to say no."

"But I go all soft inside, Sam, and everybody knows it. And kids always ask me for favors."

"I know, Ada. I was soft in first grade. Then I took a chance and said no and now they don't ask me anymore."

My mind retreats to something vaguely pleasant. I am the shortest girl in my third-grade class and I am as soft as you can get. We are sitting on a rug and there's a substitute teacher in front of the room. Nobody can calm down. Kids are throwing airplanes, yelling to each other, making fun of the sub. By accident I fart and the kids burst out laughing. Later, the substitute is completely fed up. She tells everyone to write, "I will not torment my substitute teacher" two hundred times for homework. Two boys from my class go to the front of the room, and I hear parts of a conversation. "She hasn't done anything wrong. You shouldn't make her do it," and suddenly the substitute teacher is in front of me. "Your classmates think you should be the only one who doesn't have to write sentences tonight. What do you think?" I don't know what to say. I am overcome with gratitude.

Retrogression 40:
September 15, 2007, 6:59 p.m.

The man moves quickly in our direction. He doesn't smile. I can't engage him. I thank him again. This time, I'm uncertain why I am thanking him.

Chapter 40: Spring Thaw

I have been reading *The Rural Life* by Verlyn Klinkenborg, and his descriptions of winter bring back the successions of New England winters of my childhood—the gnarled earth, the frozen topsoil. By my early forties, the frozen layers are finally ready for a deep thaw.

We are at parents' night and Arne and I are discussing Ada. She is having trouble with math. I enjoy talking with Arne. Over the summer we spent a day at an amusement park with him and his daughters. It was a blast.

"Hey, I used to teach math," he tells me. "I'd be happy to tutor her a bit. Why doesn't she come home with Lisa tomorrow after school?"

Arne is a married stay-at-home dad, a retired schoolteacher, and everything he has done thus far has shown him to be trustworthy. It has been easy to open up to Arne. He listens well. He takes his time when he answers a question, really considering it. But I still don't like the idea of Ada spending time at his house without another adult there. In fact, the thought of it terrifies me.

"I just have to call Mark," I tell Arne, hoping Mark will find a reason why Ada can't go.

But Mark is all for it. We have run into a wall with Ada in math. She needs a new strategy.

After I hang up, I find myself objecting. "It's too much to ask," I say.

Arne doesn't agree. "I don't mind, Christine."

"Well, I have a meeting tomorrow, but I'd like to be there to see what you do," I say.

Arne promises to talk with me about math strategies when I pick up Ada after my meeting. I'm out of excuses. I agree.

"So Ada will take the bus with Lisa tomorrow afternoon," I say.

"Yes," he says.

As we exit the school, I think of my friend Manu, who has no problem asking parents if they have guns in their houses. If they do, her children can't play there. Manu and I both have soft hearts. We don't want to hurt anyone. When I want to feel good about myself, she's the one I call, but when it comes to her children, she will do anything, even if it hurts someone else. I never quite got this until I had children of my own. Thinking of Manu renews my resolve.

Arne begins to walk away and I follow him. There's no deliberation, no thought involved, no agonizing about hurt feelings, even though what I'm about to say will be one of the harshest things I've ever said.

"Arne," I say hoarsely. "I need to talk."

He turns toward me and stops, waiting. We're alone for a second.

"This isn't about you," I begin. "It has nothing to do with you. It's my problem," I say. "I was molested as a child. So I never allow Ada to go to a house unless there are two adults there."

He looks at me, confused, perhaps stunned.

"It's not that I don't trust you. It's that I don't trust anyone." Arne's expression sags.

"Because the man who did this to me. He was trustworthy. Everyone thought so. So now I don't trust anyone with my children."

People from parents' night begin to pour out of the school like ants, swarming on both sides of us.

"I like you too much not to be honest with you," I say.

Arne blinks a few times.

The PTA ex-president, a woman with long, red hair, stops to talk with Arne, and he has to compose himself quickly. By the time Arne turns back to me, he has figured out what to say.

"You're telling me you have some baggage, right?"

"Yes," I say.

"I could say I understand how you feel, but I don't," Arne tells me. "I've never experienced what you did. But one of the reasons I like you is that I always know where I stand with you. Sometimes in the South, somebody can be smiling at you but underneath they're pissed and you wouldn't even know it. But you're real."

"Thanks," I say.

"Maybe you need to do this. Look, there will be two adults in the house. Lisa's tutor will be there. And you can call Ada and ask her how she is if you like. In fact, you probably should. I know this won't help, but I'm not a child molester."

"I know," I say. "Most people aren't."

When I pick up Ada the next day, she is wearing a princess tiara, playing with Lisa in an upstairs room. Arne and I speak awkwardly at first, but this melts away. He takes me on a tour of his house. My hands shake and my head hurts, the result of a day of defrosting. Even though it's September, I can feel the spring thaw as it works through me from the inside out.

The years of cold unstiffen at my core—sweat under my arms, perspiration on the sides of my legs and in the crevices of my elbows, softening outward, and droplets forming in the corners of my eyes, ready to fall and sink into the soft dirt.

Retrogression 41:

September 15, 2007,

6:58 p.m. and 32 seconds.

I see the man walking toward us and acknowledge him with a nod. He's coming to help with the cart. "Thank you," I say and smile.

Chapter 41: My Writing Circle

We're sitting at Starbucks. Ada has a box of crayons next to her and is drawing a picture of me with huge hair, a skirt, droopy lids, and a stick-thin body. I have two tears running down my face and am surrounded by people going "AAAAAAAAAAA." The caption: "Mom and The Bad Hiar [sic] day." Denise is across from me smiling. She has white teeth and brown eyes. She has a smile that takes over her entire face and long dreadlocks, for which she carries a poem with her at all times called "My Locks." She has just purchased yogurt for both of us with granola and honey in it. For this meeting, Denise has read and commented on my story "Search Terms" about lesbians from the South who felt marginalized by white culture. She says, "See, white people have the weirdest discussions. Black people would never have these types of conversations." Then she tells me an animated story. You'd never know once upon a time she could barely move—lupus—the subject of her novel.

She says, "Okay, so everything about this guy looks white. He's white. He has blue eyes. He has blond hair. But he dresses in Kofi hats, uses hip slang, and tells everyone he is black. I say to him, 'But look at you. You could pass as white. Life's easier when you're white. Why are you making things so difficult on yourself?' 'Because the best part of me is black,' he says. 'It's the part I love the most.'"

Ada looks up from her drawing and stares at Denise. Her blue eyes shine.

Maisa and I are talking on the phone. I have just finished giving her feedback on an article she's writing about labor photographers, and she's describing the exhibition that displays their photographs in a New York library. Her article is edgy and personal. I have known Maisa since I was in undergraduate school and she is, in every way except by birth, a sister. She is strikingly beautiful—brown eyes and hair, red lipstick, and stylish, colorful clothes. We begin to talk about one of the stories in this book, "Waiting for Repairs." At this point, my ending is different. It's artificial. It doesn't fully explain my connection with the computer repairman.

"Christine, maybe it's because I'm brown, you know, but I had a really hard time with this story. Plus, I hate it when people bring up 9/11 and don't put it into a larger context. I mean we've perpetrated all kinds of atrocities. We've killed countless innocent Iraqis, tortured people, so the revisiting of 9/11 doesn't really work for me."

"I'm not sure how to end it," I admit.

"Christine, this story has no trace of you in it at all. When I read it, I feel as though it was written by Fox News, not you. There's something in here, some connection, that's missing."

"I agree, but this is what happened. I feel terrible about

it. But I'm feeling so vulnerable these days I'm creating these crazy scenarios. It really bothers me."

"Well, what part of the scenario is it that you fear the most?"

"It's the going to jail part," I say. "It's such a loss of control and it has happened to innocent people before. Have you ever seen that movie with Trapper John, or is it B.J. Hunnicutt, from *M*A*S*H*, who plays this man who sold flowers? He's tried for a murder he never committed. It ruins his life. He gets a divorce. Nobody wants to hire him." As soon as I say this, the absurdity of the example I use hits me full force. In Georgia, Troy Davis is one of many black men who are on death row with negligible evidence against them, but all I can think of is a fictional white man.

"So it's going to jail that you fear," Maisa says, interrupting my thoughts. "It's not this man."

I think for a moment and relief sweeps over me. I am afraid of losing control. Maybe this man and his vulnerabilities remind me of my own, Maisa and I wonder. Now I can write the ending.

I'm at Eliza's house. We are drinking tea and eating popcorn from Trader Joe's. Eliza is over-the-top about Trader Joe's. She can't stand it that she's made this discovery.

"I said, 'Oh, I don't know. It can't be that good.' But then I went to the store and bought a few things and really, everything I buy there is excellent."

We can see Eliza's beautiful garden through the large back windows of her house. She has done everything herself, from planting, to maintaining, to watching it all grow. It's one of the things she's most proud of.

Eliza is a Pulitzer Prize–winning reporter from the *New York Times* who has just finished a book about the great migration of black Americans from the South to the North. Her book is so delicious, even though the subject matter is raw and difficult to hear about, and I have fallen in love with the three main characters as they struggle through their transplanted northern lives, overcoming incredible obstacles. By this point, I have had all 544 pages read to me, one of the most decadent things I have allowed myself to do in years. But now Eliza is asking me about my day.

"I went to the Elementary School Roundup with Samuel today, but I felt like such an outsider. I remember going to Ada's roundup two years ago and we had a blast. They take you on the bus and you meet all your kid's teachers. But now I feel so different from the other parents, like I don't want to be near them. And then I found myself talking about the attack with someone I barely know when she asked me why I was on leave this semester."

"Oh, Christine. You don't have to tell anybody about the reason for your leave. For all they know, you are on leave to do research. It's true, your research is on your children."

"Yes, but I'm on a committee with this woman and I haven't been to any of the meetings. I just thought she'd understand me better."

"Christine, you still want to please people. I was like that, too. It doesn't matter what anybody thinks about this. And they'll never understand you. They just won't."

"Lots of people are telling me to move on."

"Maybe it's not time to move on, but they'll never understand that. Maybe you don't want to move on."

"Maybe I don't. I don't want to move on. Well, not until I've finished this book."

What an odd statement for me to say, I think as I am saying it. But there is something so riveting, so real, so in the moment, raw, and authentic about living here.

Felix, Eliza, and I are sitting at Method Café, and I have just ordered a divine chocolate drink. Eliza has a cookie with almonds in it she's made us try, and Felix is drinking a tea he has poured from a steeping pot. We have already broken two glass containers since we began meeting here for our writing group, and we wonder if this place is too posh for us. Felix is an ichnologist, a man who my son cannot stop talking about, even though they've only met once. His book has coached me on how to notice and appreciate the living world my children explore and discover naturally. Because I have recounted Felix's animal life-or-death scenarios to my children, my son wants to be an ichnologist. I now know what a trace is, understand where to find the cave of an ant lion, and can identify roach (blattoidean) traces (dung) on my front porch. Felix's descriptions of animal and plant traces on the Georgia coast were just what my children and I needed to reconnect to our own backyard.

Felix is reading about finding a horseshoe crab washed up on the beach. Usually, by the time they are lying flat on the sand, they're dead, but Felix makes a discovery through examining the traces the crab has left in the sand. He turns to his friend and says to him, "I think she's still alive."

Eliza and I gasp. Although Felix's colleague is more interested in his field notes than a live specimen, he decides to humor Felix. Suddenly it becomes a rescue mission rather than two ichnologists looking to resolve a crime scene. They pick up the horseshoe crab and run with it to the water. Sure enough, the horseshoe crab moves as Felix sings "Born Free" into the wind.

Eliza and I are talking about "Intuition."

"Christine, I don't like this story," she tells me.

"Why?" I ask.

Christine Ristaino   199

We're sitting on her couch. In between us is a beautiful white Havanese named Sonia who is on her back wanting to have her stomach rubbed. She is tiny, friendly, and seems to be smiling, if a dog can smile. Eliza shifts in her seat.

"Well, first of all, this man is guilty without a trial. Do you realize most people are killed by a spouse or a significant other, not by a stranger? And you even said in the story about your husband that black people usually kill black people and white people usually kill white people. But here you are saying this man is guilty."

"Well, he returned to the crime scene later in the day with his friends and her key so they could rob more things," I tell her.

"So he's a thief. That doesn't mean he murdered her," Eliza says.

"But I read in the paper his fingerprints were all over the object that killed her," I tell Eliza, certain this is enough evidence.

"And many black people would say the police planted them there," Eliza tells me.

Eliza points to her own research. "Do you know how many times black people have been killed or jailed for even looking at a white woman? There's a history here," she says.

"In the story I was trying to show I wasn't afraid of somebody because of his race but more because I felt fear inside based on something else, something intangible but more accurate—more a gut feeling. In the past I've ignored my gut feelings. But now I listen," I say.

Eliza nods. She understands. But I have fallen short. "I'm not saying he's guilty or not guilty. It's just that due process has to occur before we can decide. Due process is part of the American system, and it should be played out. And you never focus on the age of this guy, only on his color. If anything, his age is a better indicator. He's in his early twenties, so how could he afford a posh apartment in Buckhead?"

"You're right," I say.

Eliza nods. "That's why I think you should get rid of this story altogether," she says. "Because it's not getting your point across."

Rose and I are talking on the phone. She's a college friend, the daughter of a preacher, and during my freshman year she kept me in line. Even now I find she is doing this. She has read my book. I sit at my kitchen table and listen. "Christine," she says. "The ending of your book is about found and lost voices. When you said you had been attacked, I prayed, 'Please don't let him be black' and you probably noticed I was very quiet on the other end of the phone when you told me he was. But you have to understand. Yes, black men have been treated poorly and endured slavery, and have lived difficult lives as you point out, but ultimately each individual makes his own decisions. When we look at the people in your book, the ones who hurt you, it's not about being black or white: it's about the decisions they made. And maybe that's what we all need to talk about next."

I'm at Denise's house and we have just discussed two chapters from our books. I'm about to leave and pick up my children from school.

"Denise," I say. "Could I have a copy of the poem you carry around about your locks? I'm referencing it in my book."

Denise begins to laugh and I have trouble bringing her back to the conversation since every time she begins to talk, she laughs again. "Are you kidding? You think I bring that poem around with me? It's my book's protagonist who carries it. I wrote that poem for her. She's my character, not me."

Retrogression 42:
September 15, 2007,
6:58 p.m. and 12 seconds.

When I reach the sidewalk and the wheels become stuck on the curb, the man on the bench stands and walks in our direction.

Chapter 42:
Haunts

Ronnie and I have shared our books with each other. Despite the fact he's writing fiction with characters that have supernatural qualities and killer dogs appearing at the first sign of trouble and then disappearing into the realm of the dead, our books are remarkably similar. The grandmother figure in Ronnie's book is quirky and strong. There are children whose innocence is destroyed by child abductors and molesters. Fear, racism, and violence weave sinuously through every interaction, with disastrous repercussions.

Ronnie discusses my chapter "Misunderstanding," where I admit that bathing my children unnerves me.

"This, for me, is the most important chapter," he says. "I was wondering when you would reveal how your experience with the man has affected you. I have been wanting to know. For me, this chapter is key."

"How so?" I ask.

"Well, you show how the sins of our ancestors can be passed from generation to generation, like the effects of alcoholism on you and your friend, Natalie. This story shows the repercussions of a singular event."

"I hadn't connected the two stories you mention," I say. "I love that they connect in this way. I guess the man does haunt my children, doesn't he?"

"Yes," Ronnie states and it's the first time I realize just how much.

I'm not afraid of the man. He is dead. But from the grave, like the protagonist in Ronnie's book, he haunts us. He has made me afraid for my children. I fear for their peace of mind—that I could ruin it in a single act by doing something stupid or unforgivable, or by leaving them, by dying on them. I could open my mouth and say cruel words, or get into a car and drive away, or take my hand and do unforgiveable things to them, too horrible to put down on paper or even imagine.

I am happy for my busy life—raising children, teaching classes, scheduling appointments with students and colleagues, long hours of repetitive math sheets and spelling words with the kids, innumerable tasks and busywork. I forget for minutes, hours at a time, but my full days do nothing to restore my peace of mind. Somewhere on this planet, in this world, maybe this city, perhaps near or far away, there is a man, maybe dead or alive, a man who once sat on a bench at a shopping store waiting for us to reach the curb. My son was three years old, my daughter five, and I, a naïve forty. Perhaps that mild September evening, my children, too, lost this vital peace.

Retrogression 43:
September 15, 2007,
6:58 p.m. and 10 seconds.

By now we're almost to the sidewalk, very close to the entrance, but slightly to the right of it. The parking lot is well-lit. There are lots of parked cars, but it's surprisingly quiet and I don't see anybody around except the man on the bench.

Chapter 43:
Climbing Up and Out

I don't notice haircuts or new clothes or hoop earrings. My father once shaved off his beard and it took me two days to realize. But I can remember entire conversations, or the moment when I felt valued by somebody, or when I first loved a person for something he or she said or did. During the first month of classes each semester, I remember the conversations I have with my students. I relish them, but I have no idea who said what until much later on, when I've finally placed faces with actions and ideas. Until then, my students' words float around me like beautiful, stunning jewels.

Ever since I told my family and friends about the man, I have felt exposed. I realize this vulnerability opens me up to possibility. I am certain I'll have an opportunity to climb up. The knowledge of this future climb helps me. I know I will not always seem so small, be so hard on myself, feel like I'm doing everything wrong, that everything won't seem like a crisis. I know this because I have been here before and then climbed up and out to see the sun.

Life is stressful at home. This week my husband and I have a terrible fight—layered, harsh, unbearable, necessary. "I know you want to save the world, that the things you're doing with schools and for your students make you feel good. But I look at you and you are exhausted and you come home with nothing left," my husband says when I accuse him of being angry and unreachable. He is right and wrong at the same time.

Today Ronnie and I sit at a unique restaurant that mixes it all up—pasta with vindaloo sauce is my absolute favorite. I focus on a section of his chapter where a white person tries to make the main character, Clyde, feel good by saying his father doesn't view Clyde as black even though he is. Clyde says in a tongue-in-cheek manner that this statement by his friend "was supposed to be soothing." I tell Ronnie about my student. She is Korean and her boyfriend is a white student from the South. Often people tell her she and her boyfriend will one day have cute kids. My student sees this as a balm, an "I accept your relationship so much I think your kids will be cute." But she feels as though they are reducing what she has with her boyfriend to genetics. "Who says I want to get married and have kids in the first place?" she asks. "People don't say that to white couples." I bring up my reservations when people call me vertically challenged. "People feel they're being sensitive to my height when they say this," I tell Ronnie. "But really they're expressing discomfort. What's wrong with being short? What's wrong with being black? What's wrong with a Korean college student dating someone who is white? It's as though it's so bad they have to call it something else. They think they're giving a compliment, but they're really saying they don't accept it."

This conversation is still in the air when Ronnie says, "Do you relate to Clyde?"

"Yes," I say. "What's strange is that until you remind me, I keep imagining him as a white man." Deep inside I feel an ache, as though I've said something wrong. "I mean, I don't know why I don't remember this information," I say. "Maybe I know it for a while but then I forget."

Ronnie begins to talk about something else, but I take us back to this topic. I'm panicking now, afraid I've said something offensive. I can't quite put my finger on why it feels bad to me, so I just keep saying more.

"I don't know, Ronnie. The fact that I don't remember he's black, do you think that's a problem? I mean, shouldn't I know all the time? Like I know he's connected to supernaturals and I know he's Scottish because the grandmother and kids are always speaking in a Scottish brogue. But the fact that he's black . . ."

Ronnie lists a number of times when he has conveyed that Clyde is black throughout the book, and I realize he's told his reader quite often. But this isn't the first time I've missed critical information like this during my lifetime. *What's wrong with my brain?* I wonder. And Alzheimer's does come to mind as a viable option.

Finally, Ronnie pauses and looks at me. "Isn't this similar to what we were just talking about, the balm?"

I get Ronnie's reference and think of the line, "I doubt my father views you as black." Isn't what I said to him another version of that?

"You're right," I say to Ronnie. "It's similar. I've done the same thing."

"So do you want me to give you stereotypical behavior so it will be more obvious that he's black?" Ronnie asks, and his tone is patient.

"No," I say.

Ronnie begins to talk about Spycer, a violent force in his book. "You can't forget he's black," Ronnie says. "I don't," I respond, but as I say this, I know it's not true. Despite the many references to his race, even some in this chapter, I remember that he's sinister, but not black. "Sully, the magician," Ronnie says, "he demonstrates some stereotypes, too. In fact, he's the sibling who relates the most to his black identity. And of course, the father's actions recall stereotypes so it's more obvious he's black." I stare at Ronnie, searching for this information in my brain, wondering if I look like my dog, who stares at me blankly when I tell her we will be home again in the afternoon, as though we had never left the house before and then never returned. And when Ronnie mentions the white supremacist character, I realize I have forgotten this information about him, too.

I can't hear the other people in the restaurant, although there are plenty of them. The world seems small, just Ronnie and me, and I have lost myself in this conversation. I don't know if there's something wrong with my brain or if there's just too much going on in my life, but despite all the clues, I can't remember anybody's race in his book until they arrive home, open the door, walk into the house again, and remind me. "Oh yes," I say each time. And every day, when I get home in the evening, my dog jumps up and down, remembering after a long day that I exist.

Strangely enough, Ronnie's book is all about race. There are discussions about race at every turn, on every page. I remember them. They are the conversations that hit me the most, but when I am involved in the characters' day-to-day, their race somehow is the last thing I think about.

When I return home, I tell Mark about my conversation with Ronnie.

"Sweetie, everyone has a conception of what it means to be black. It doesn't mean every black man fits into your conception. That doesn't mean you're racist. It's an interesting conversation to have, actually. What makes a written character black? How do you convey that in a book without presenting stereotypes? But what you said wasn't bad. You were just trying to answer those questions."

"But what I said bothered me. I was offended by it," I tell him.

"You offended yourself?" he says and laughs.

After a number of hours I finally understand what happened. It occurs to me I don't have a visual to remind me of how Ronnie's characters look. I think of my father, beardless at the kitchen table for two full days and I remember why I forget. I don't remember because it's not what I'm looking for.

After I write this piece, I cling to this rationale for years. It comforts me, makes me feel better about myself, but in the end I realize it's only a balm as well. The reality is, I'm so programmed that even after acknowledging the world's prejudices, looking them straight in the eye, and saying they exist, even then, after twenty minutes I allow them to take over my speech, perhaps not even realizing they have taken over until years later.

Retrogression 44:

September 15, 2007,

6:58 p.m. and 7 seconds.

A man sits on a bench, his legs open, his arms dangling in between. He watches us.

Chapter 44: Twins

The kids and I are in the car on the way to school, and I'm unsure how I'll get through the day. I've been telling the whole world about memories that are so personal, scenes I've kept inside for most of my life. I'm wondering if I'm ready to be open like this.

Sam is thinking. He won't talk, won't put on his seat belt, that is, until I raise my voice. Then he quietly does. Just when I think he's never going to talk again, his sweet little voice emerges.

"I wonder what it's like to be inside an egg," he says.

"It's not like anything," Ada says. "You don't know you're there and you don't know you're not there."

"Or what it's like to be in a womb," he continues.

"The same," Ada responds.

They begin to talk about their friends, Claude and Jenny, twins. Claude spent a number of months crushed by his sister in the womb, and somehow my children know this about him.

"And Jenny was sitting on Claude and she didn't even

know it," Sam says and laughs. "I wonder if that's why Claude tortures Jenny now."

"I know," Ada says. "But that's not right."

"But Ada," Sam says. "Jenny crushed Claude. He couldn't breathe. It's life's revenge."

"You know, Sam, when you're fantastically scientific I'm so proud of you. I mean I love you. You're family. You could be being so great and then your evil side shows up. When you're being scientific or sweet, I'm so happy I have you. But with your evil side, when you annoy me, I ask myself why I have to have a brother."

"That's just my nature," Sam says.

"I know. You're right. And I can annoy you, too. But when you annoy me, I feel myself reach to your evil side, just like when you strike a match, and then I ignite like a fire, and you can't stop me then."

We arrive at the kids' school and they climb out of the car, barely aware I'm there. In class it's hard to teach. I feel awkward in front of twenty-seven students while in this funk. But as the day progresses, I'm reminded of why I do this. My student, Bao, shows up in my office with his parents. They have beautiful gifts for me—a purse from China and a gorgeous frog bookmark made of metal. Bao's parents hug me and in broken English tell me Bao loves my class. And later I see Micaela, who has a seminar right after I teach, and she blows me a kiss from across the room. And then two students, minutes apart, burst into my office and tell me they have figured out what they want to do with their lives.

Retrogression 45:

September 15, 2007, 6:58 p.m.

It's nice out, slightly windy, but warm, and we talk and joke around as we make our way toward the store entrance in the middle of the American South.

Chapter 45: Rupert

As I fly over the ocean to Saint Croix from Atlanta, I am told by two passengers not to leave my hotel. The first is a man who has lived in Saint Croix most of his life. The second, an island woman, says I'm not safe. She tears off a piece of paper from a gum wrapper and writes her phone number on it with my pen. "Enjoy the rest of the week by the television," she tells me. "Don't go out. There's too much crime out there and you stick out like a sore thumb."

Joyce, a school administrator from Saint Croix, picks me up at the airport.

"A man on the plane told me to stay in my room and a woman said to watch TV and not go out," I tell her. She admits that Saint Croix has its underbelly, but she has been living here for years. As we drive, she says, "The first two years were challenging. Nobody wanted me here and they made it clear. At the end of the second year, I called in all the parents for a general meeting. They thought I was going to resign, but instead I took a different approach. 'Have a good look at me,' I said to them.

'I am white and I'm not from here. And in August, when I return, I will still be white and not from here.'"

"Did anything change?" I ask.

"Yes," Joyce says. "Maybe they saw I understood them—that I cared about their children. I don't know. It was easier to talk with parents after that. It felt like they pulled the race card less. They no longer blamed me for their children's shortcomings. Part of it was just calling their bluff, nicely getting in their faces and calling them on their own prejudices. I earned their respect," she says.

Six months before my trip to Saint Croix, I had written to the Freedom Writers Organization. Joyce and six others had agreed to read my manuscript. Joyce shared my work with her students. The subject matter caught their interest, and she received a grant to create skits about prejudice and racism.

As we drive, Joyce tells me about the schools in Saint Croix, the customs and music of the island, her students and the skits they have written. The next day I visit three schools with a hip-hop educator named Ryan and his music producer Zeke. Although he now lives in New York, Ryan has been working with Joyce for years, and his mother still lives on the island. Ryan is a hip-hop artist, a producer, and an actor, but his ability to work with children and bring out their creative sides through hip-hop music makes him an incredible educator, too. Ryan manages to get students talking about what really matters to them, practically without them even realizing. I tag along, watching as scenes come together with messages about identity and overcoming racism. Two groups have written me into their scripts. In one I am an oppressive boss. In another, I walk to my car, unaware I'm about to be attacked by a woman who is undergoing a gang initiation.

The students from the Saint Croix schools are mostly Afro-Caribbean. Some of them are very young—between second and fifth grade—and over-the-top excited about what they are doing. They joke around and tell me all about their lives on the island. The two groups of students who have written me into their scripts are teenagers from a private school on top of a hill. There are two white girls but most students are black. Some are studying for a math test or worrying about it. Others are thrilled they got out of school to do this project.

The private school on the hill with small wooden buildings contrasts with the large, brick school I visit right after, where students explode into a fight in the halls. At this school I can barely move and students yell over each other to be heard. I can tell most of them want to talk, some about difficult topics, others about sports and cell phones, clubs and friends, homework, tests, Saint Croix, love. Their skits come together quickly.

One teenaged boy has written a soliloquy from the perspective of an elderly man. He talks about the pain he experiences because people don't trust him, automatically categorizing him as a potential child molester because he's old. He longs to have meaningful conversations with young people, but nobody will engage with him.

One of the most powerful hours of my visit takes place at the end of the second day at a local recording studio. An incarcerated youth named Rupert records a rap song he has written in response to two of my stories, while an armed guard stands two feet away from him. The song is from his perspective as a person who committed robbery and assault. "I never meant to hurt you," he sings, looking right at me, as though he was the one who had assaulted me. Afterward, the two of us speak about his talent and his plans for the future. Rupert is on the cusp of a new life, about to be released from jail.

During my stay in Saint Croix, I visit seven schools and meet hundreds of children. I attend a Michael Jackson Halloween party the night before I return to Atlanta. Joyce, Ryan, and Zeke never stop moving. They dance, give awards for the best costumes and dancers, crack jokes. Joyce is crazy funny. She'll do just about anything, and everything she does models what it means to live out your philosophy of life, not just dream about it. I spend most of the party on the sidelines learning about the parents and children of this community. On the last day of my visit, I drive through the hot streets of Saint Croix with Ryan and Zeke as we film final scenes and say goodbye to the children. And then Joyce is taking me to the airport.

I bring home CDs of beautiful music from the Virgin Islands—calypso beats, hometown reggae, and songs sung by the children I visited. When Rupert's rap songs arrive in my mailbox months later, my own children can't believe it.

"Mom, did he really write these songs because he read your book?" Ada asks me.

"Well, he read part of it," I say.

"Wow, Mom. You got him to write music!" she says.

But with the CD comes the worst possible news about Rupert. Joyce tells me that for the first three months after Rupert's release from jail, he took classes and did well. But then he began spending time with his old crowd.

"He was killed by a friend," Joyce writes. "Wasted potential."

I don't tell my children about Rupert. I want so much for them to believe Rupert had changed, that all it takes is for one person to believe in us.

Retrogression 46:
September 15, 2007, 6:57 p.m.

My children and I find a child's cart in the parking lot. They climb in and I begin pushing. My curly hair blows comfortably in the breeze, lifting and settling every few seconds near the sides of my face.

Chapter 46: How to Save a Life

For anyone who has been attacked, there's an anxiety that circulates just below the surface. If you turn the corner too quickly, hear a book drop, or catch a shadow on your wall, the man who attacked you is right there. During the first few years after my attack, I turn the corner to see my attacker thousands of times in the quiet of my own house, only to find that a book has shimmied off the washing machine during the spin cycle, or the shadow of a head on the wall is just a house plant with lots of leaves, or the black streak to the side of me is my own eyes, playing tricks.

During this period, Ada and Samuel seem to suffer from the same fears. They worry the bad guy from the store will come to our house.

"We've changed our locks," I say. "It would be hard for him to get in."

But my uncertainty, my inability to give them absolutes, makes the conversation escalate.

"What if that bad guy breaks a window and gets in? Breaks it with a stick and hurts us?" Sam asks.

"I will always try to protect you," I respond.

That much is true. But I can never give them the answer they want, can never promise eternal and absolute protection. How can I? So they talk about protecting me instead.

Yet there are fleeting moments when I feel we're accomplishing the impossible. One day I overhear Samuel and Ada talking about his nightly visits to my room. "When I feel scared, I come here. This is the only place I don't feel scared," he tells Ada.

And my mother reminds me of the hours she once spent by my bedside reciting prayers of protection after a neighbor had committed suicide. Although I remember the comfort that came with saying the rosary with my mother, the reason behind this nightly ritual had eluded me.

Although most people suggest we stop coddling Samuel and let him cry it out for a few nights alone in his bedroom, Mark and I do everything we can to comfort him. If I often wake startled and jump up to check on the children, we reason Samuel, too, could be feeling this type of fear. So we tell him he must do what he needs to feel safe again at night. Sometimes we find him in his sister's room, with a pillow and a blanket, stretched on the floor, a teddy bear under each armpit and a hand holding tightly on to the ruffle of her bed. But most nights, I bring my laptop into my bedroom and Samuel sneaks in beside me, curling into my side like a small cat might. Later, my husband joins us and for the rest of the night the three of us share our marital bed, my son and I curled up together, and my husband's arm thrown over my shoulder, his hand gently touching mine.

Ada is taking a shower when I notice it. I peek in to hand her some soap and there's a huge bulge in the right groin area. I imagine it's a tumor, but instead, she has a hernia there, and two others I hadn't seen.

Christine Ristaino   221

I make the surgery appointment right away. I don't want to think about it for too long. Mark takes the day off, we drive her to a hospital thirty minutes away, check her in, go through an efficient process of bureaucracy and pre-op, and then Mark and I are in the waiting room and Ada is in surgery.

For those who have had to wait for a child to come out of surgery, you know. It's not until the doctor enters the waiting room with a practiced, reassuring smile, that you can stop putting out of your mind the worst-case scenarios laid out for you on the waiver form.

Going into surgery for Ada is an adventure. She has read the Madeline book. She knows about the gifts and the scar she'll be able to show like a badge of honor to her friends at school. What she doesn't know about are the post-op tears every parent and child seem to experience.

"You might have a little bit of pain afterward," I try to warn her on the way there. "I know, Mom," she replies.

Ada's adventure starts out the way our visit to the store began. It is playful and fun. She is relaxed and enjoying herself as she is visited by doctors, nurses, anesthesiologists, big burly men who are to wheel her into the operating room. She smiles at them, laughs at their jokes, introduces them to her new stuffed fish, Elly, whom she says is a boy and not a girl every time one of them refers to him as "she." When they wheel Ada out to the unknown, the whole surgical crew—doctors, nurses, anesthesiologist, and bed movers—are around her asking questions, joking with her, and laughing as they push the bed. Ada continues to entertain them by putting the mask over her fish's mouth so he can fall asleep first, since he's going to have his appendix taken out at the same time.

My husband and I stay in the OR waiting room, newcomers to this world. I have my computer so I can come up with titles for a few of my stories from this book, since an agent is interested in reading it. My work does little to comfort me. I can't help but think of the worst-case scenario. My daughter could be allergic to the anesthesia and die on the operating table while my husband and I sit silently in the waiting room reading. We could survive the operation only to be in a terrible accident on the way home, my son orphaned. Once home, Ada could roughhouse too much with her brother and rip open the stitches.

After the surgeon tells us Ada has done fine, a nurse walks us back to see her. When we arrive, Ada is leaning to one side of the bed, sobbing.

"Mommy, help me," she keeps saying over and over again.

The last time she cried this much was in the parking lot. While then I had tried to hide my bloody face from her, in this crisis I climb into her bed and put my arms around her.

"I'm here," I tell her as I rub her back.

When our stay is over, a nurse places Ada on my lap and wheels us out.

"Ada," I say. "The last time I was wheeled out of a hospital with you on my lap, you were a newborn baby."

This leads to the first post-surgery smile I see out of Ada. It will be a few more days before the familiar smile visits us again.

I spend the week carrying Ada from room to room, reading her books, and chatting about the world. Then, just as Ada begins to go for longer stretches without pain medicine, she spikes a high fever and seems to fall back into infancy.

When your children are babies, you admire every inch of them—fingers, toes, eyes, the curve of their nose, the lobe of each ear, their long, curling eyelashes, their flushed, red cheeks. Once they are in kinetic motion, you stop doing this. They are a lovable storm whirling by you. But when they are sick, feverish and burning up in your arms, you notice how they have grown. You see their baby eyes, those same ones you used to look into as they gulped down breast milk. You recognize a pin-sized white spot on the cartilage of their ear. You put your hand to their burning forehead, feel its baby smoothness. You let their hand grip a finger until they drift off to sleep in your arms. You forget what they feel like sleeping on your shoulder until their temperature reads 104 degrees, and then you cling to them as they sleep heavily in your arms.

Ada sleeps in my arms for three days and suddenly I am her mother again. As I rock and hold her, I think of a CD a student of mine had given me. His campus group had remade a song by The Fray, "How to Save a Life." In the song, a camp counselor asks how to save a child whose life has gone terribly wrong. "I would have stayed up all night had I known how to save a life." *Could he have saved this child's life?* I wonder. Is there ever a way to know how? As I nurse my daughter back to health, as I rock her, tell her I love her, hold her close so I can inhale the familiar scent of her shampoo, I realize perhaps I can save my children—some of the time.

Retrogression 47:
September 15, 2007, 6:56 p.m.

We see the store sign in the distance. I put on my blinker, turn into the parking lot, find a spot close to the store, and help the kids climb out of the car. We hold hands and walk toward the bright entrance.

Chapter 47: Spelling Bee

Two of my students invite me to a play they are in called *Spelling Bee*. "Can I bring my daughter?" I ask them.

They reserve two tickets.

It is a northeasterly cold night and halfway there Ada has to use the bathroom, which tips our arrival time to almost late. We run into a restaurant, and she pulls down her pants as she enters the stall, almost tripping over her pant leg. Afterward, she stands daydreaming by the faucet.

"Wash your hands, Ada," I say. "Or we'll be late."

When we arrive, I grab Ada's hand and we race toward the building. The cold wind slaps our faces, and we sing the theme to the Lone Ranger to help distract us from the cold. As we enter the building, I see Ronnie Bonner and a teacher I know. I stop singing. They smile. Okay, so I have been singing the theme to the Lone Ranger. It's no big deal.

My students play spelling bee competitors. One wears a display of feathers and homemade tan overalls. The other, more prim and proper, loses the spelling bee because he has an erection. Ada doesn't get the less than subtle humor, but she is all over everything else, laughing and carrying on even during serious parts. We are like two schoolchildren, giggling and entertaining the whole aisle behind us. The audience loves Ada. Some pat her on the head. I even catch smiles from the actors when they hear her delight.

I find I am drawn into the plot, unable to spell any of the words, but caught in the emotional dramas that surround each spelling competitor's life. At the end of the play, Olive, a shy girl whose parents are absent from the bee, sings to her mother, pleading with her to participate in her life. Tears stream down Ada's face. We hold hands, cling to each other.

Once the play is over, Ada and I sneak out quietly. It's past both our bedtimes, and it's dark and cold outside. Our car feels miles away. I hold Ada's hand as we jog toward the car, our breath in front of us, leading the way. I unlock quickly, open Ada's door, and buckle her in, imagining at any second somebody could jump us. Nobody does. Soon all the car doors are locked and the heat fills our car with comforting warmth.

Retrogression 48:
September 15, 2007, 6:49 p.m.

"We should be going," I say to my friend Joan. "Samuel's getting so big he needs a new car seat. You're getting big, Sam!" My son pulls at my arm. "Yeah, Mom. Let's go get me a new chair!" he says, punctuating the word "new." "Can I have one, too?" Ada asks. "No, sweetie. You got a new one last year." "Don't worry, Ada," Sam says. "I'll share mine with you."

Chapter 48: Women in Parking Lots

I am going to get my eye scraped. There has been a large, transparent bubble in the corner of my left eye for about a year and a half now, and I'm about to have it removed. When I first discovered it, I was in my car. I turned quickly and caught it in my rearview mirror. I decided to pull over and have a better look. In the parking lot, I saw a doctor I knew, the real-life inspiration for the movie character Doc Hollywood. He was standing in front of a copy center, his hair all over the place like Einstein's. I parked my car and approached him. He had just photocopied a manuscript he had written that discussed every malady on the face of this earth in layman's terms. He showed it to me. I showed him my eye. He spent fifteen minutes in the parking lot trying to figure out what it was, his hands practically in my eyes and my head leaning to one side.

Doc Hollywood and I concluded I needed to see an eye doctor. The doctor sent me to a specialist who drained the bubble a number of times, but it continued to refill. After months of this routine, the specialist sent me to a surgeon to cut the bubble out.

When I arrive at the surgeon's office, I park my car on the tenth floor of the parking deck and begin to walk in the direction of the exit. As I draw closer, I notice a woman in front of the door that leads to both the stairwell and the elevator. Immediately she engages my glance and I imagine she wants something from me.

This woman at the door unnerves me, but I am not sure where else to go. Other than walking around ten floors of parking lot, there's no alternative. I hide my wallet under my coat and move in her direction.

She is frail with blond, long hair, and it occurs to me she could be on drugs. Before I can skirt around her, she is in my face.

"I need your help," she says.

I check to see if she has anything in her hands—a knife, a gun. Can I get away easily if she grabs me?

"I need your help. I'm afraid. I have this fear of elevators. I don't expect you to understand, but could you help me get down from here?"

I hesitate.

"I am afraid of elevators," she says again. "I was hoping to park on the first floor, but there were no parking spaces."

I don't move.

"Please," she says again. "I can't walk down all those stairs. I feel like I'm going to faint. I need somebody to take me down with her in the elevator."

It happens suddenly. First, I recognize her plight. Then I know I can help her. I reach out and grab her hand. She has on red mittens. I look into her eyes and press the elevator button. We wait.

Years ago I was given a bad flu shot. For minutes I felt as though I was going to faint and then fell to the ground, stopped breathing, and had convulsions. I spent the next year afraid I would pass out. I asked strangers to help me cross the street and once crawled out of a two-hundred-person lecture class because I was sure I would drop to the floor if I stood up.

"I used to suffer from panic attacks," I tell her as we wait. "But now I don't. One day you won't either. But I do know how you feel. You think you're going to die."

"Yes," she says. "And I had to pull over twice on my way here because I was terrified I would pass out in the car. And now I'm scared to cross that bridge over the street to get to my counselor. Luckily my friend is going to meet me at the foot of the bridge."

"Just get through one thing at a time," I tell her.

"Thank you," she responds.

"I know people don't understand," I say. "They think it's all in your head, but it's not. It's in your body. It's physical. You feel like you are going to faint."

We continue to hold hands. When the elevator arrives, we step into it together. It's at this point I know for sure: it's my own hand I'm holding, my own heart I now comfort, yet from another place.

We are all the same, I think. *If only we would talk to each other like we do in a crisis, then we would see how similar we are.*

I think of the woman at the parking lot a few years earlier. When she asked how I was, I downplayed the event, hoping she would leave.

The elevator stops on the first floor, and I continue to hold her hand until we arrive at the bridge.

"I found this guardian angel up there who helped me ride the elevator," the woman tells her friend.

"Oh really?" The friend smiles sheepishly. "Well, that was good of you," she says to me.

"I used to suffer from panic attacks and they're horrible," I say.

I turn to the blond woman. "You will get through it. One day this period of your life will be a distant memory. Just the fact you had the courage to come here today means you're going to be fine."

She lets go of my hand. As she and her friend walk away, the thought occurs to me that I should have given her my phone number, but I stop myself from following. *You did exactly what you were supposed to do*, I tell myself. *Now you need to return to your own life.*

My oculoplastic surgeon's name is Will. He has spent some time in Italy and traveled a bit. We speak about his visits abroad and his love of languages. Then he looks at my eye.

"It's just under the top white layer, but it's above the muscle," he says. "This is good. It means we don't have to do this in the hospital. We can do it right here if you'd like. In fact, do you want me to do it now?" he asks.

"Yes," I respond. "Let's get it over with."

He nods. "It's funny, the cells in your eye that produced this cyst are tear-producing cells. Those are tears in the bubble. Somehow these cells lay dormant all these years just below the surface of your eye until recently when they became active and began producing tears. I'm not sure what the catalyst could have been."

In the past I would have lunged into my story about the parking lot attack, but today I don't need to tell him.

As I sit with the doctor and joke with him while he scrapes my eye, I realize I'm brave. I'm getting my eyeball scraped. I was attacked, bruised and beaten, and I still went to work the following Monday, stood in front of three classrooms of students and told them why I looked the way I did. I carried two children through difficult pregnancies and gave birth to both of them naturally. I can now drive in the left lane on highways without having a panic attack. I'm no longer afraid of fainting. I was raped. I was molested. I can now admit these things happened.

I think about the woman in the elevator, and it occurs to me how absolutely beautiful she was in her frailty, so open, so honest about her limitations. I suddenly understand what I must have looked like to the world in my mid-twenties, when I felt the way she did. I allow myself to remember what life had been like that year. When I held the woman's hand, I told her she would be okay. Suddenly I know for sure, I will, too.

Retrogression 49:
September 15, 2007, 6:46 p.m.

The kids hug Asher, Robbie, and little Kay. "I love yittle Kay," Sam states as we walk away. "She's so cute," Ada agrees. At the door I grab the hand of Louise, the director of children's religious education. "Great night," I say. "I know," she replies. "It went well. Did you meet the new minister, Christine?" "No, he was surrounded by so many people. Maybe tomorrow after the service I'll introduce myself." "You should," she tells me. "The two of you should meet."

Chapter 49:
When All Else Fails

By the time Lara was ten, her mother, a teacher, had been a recovering stroke survivor for half of Lara's childhood. Lara's mom eventually returned to the school where she had taught, but this time as a librarian. She would never again teach. Lara was ten years old the day her father picked her up early from school. He didn't say a word, but Lara understood that a second stroke had been less forgiving: her mother was dead this time. Lara's father coped with his wife's death by having a string of girlfriends. Lara, her sister, and her brother, virtually on their own at night, drank alcohol as their family's dirty dishes piled around them. When she was fourteen, Lara's older brother ran a red light and smashed into oncoming traffic. Lara was in the car. She spent months in the hospital in a full body cast after the accident. During the first week, Lara's sister never left her side. Then she stopped visiting altogether. One afternoon a few months later, Lara's sister went to the top of an apartment building and threw herself off.

Lara began chanting with Buddhist friends. Buddhism is what saved her, made her turn from drugs and alcohol to community. Lara and I met many years later at a language school we had both worked for in Italy. We stayed in touch and I eventually recruited her to work with me in the United States, teaching Italian. After my attack, Lara invited me to chant with her. Each Wednesday morning I would go to her house and we would sit in front of the Gohonzon and recite the words Nam Myōhō Renge Kyō.

I could see why Lara had turned to Nichiren Buddhism during the worst period of her life. Every time I looked into the Gohonzon, the mandala venerated by Nichiren Buddhists, I felt a strange peace. Some days, in the outline of the letters before me that looked like human figures, I would see myself holding the hands of my children. Other days, somebody else was holding their hands, but no matter how far away I was from them, we were always connected.

Lara told me the correct place to look while chanting was directly at a heart symbol made out of letters in Sanskrit in the middle of the Gohonzon. I stared at the heart and before I knew it, my children were popping out of its center, glancing around, like two little ETs. Sometimes they were above my heart looking out with a delightful playfulness. Other times I could see them inside my heart, moving around, trying to get comfortable, like a gestation. I always saw my husband's profile right next to the heart and one of my arms extended toward him. Often the Sanskrit letters looked like labor workers with hats, their arms extended out to my children, husband, and me, and I was one of them.

Although Buddhism had saved her, by her mid-thirties Lara was still haunted by the deaths of her mother and sister. The August before I was attacked, Lara returned from a trip to Italy with a big gash in her leg after her brother had crashed the motorcycle they were on, throwing her off the bike, over a wall, and down the ravine of a cliff. My husband said Lara shouldn't drive with her brother, but I believed the real change needed to occur in the place where terrible tragedy takes up residence, close to her heart.

After I was attacked, we were the walking wounded, I with my black eye and Lara with a limp and a long scar on the side of her leg. Lara confided she chose the wrong type of men, men who were immature, claustrophobic, depressed, unfaithful—those she knew would leave her. Desperate to change this dynamic, Lara and I role-played. I was her sister.

"What do you want to say to me?" I asked.

"I miss you," she responded.

"Are you upset with me?" I said.

"Yes. Why did you have to leave? I know things weren't right, Dad was never home. But you could have told me you wanted to go."

Lara's voice cracked. Tears slid down her face.

"You could have told us. We would have all left, gone away to the beach, just the three of us, or to Spain, wherever you wanted. We were the Three Musketeers."

When Lara left for Italy a year and a half after my attack, she had severed all ties with the uncommitted men she had been dating.

"I'm still emotionally drawn to one of them even though I don't see him anymore," she said. "He's gorgeous, but that's not the reason. He's needy and I keep trying to fix him. Our relationship is like the one I had with my sister."

"That makes so much sense," I said. "You want to save him because you couldn't save her."

"You know, there are rumors my sister was raped the summer before she died. I'm going to find out more about my sister's death the next time I'm in Italy."

I, too, was changing. Self-reflection, conversations, writing it all down, had given me a new way of hearing myself in relation to others—the voices of Lara and Ada, Mark and Sam, my children's teachers, the medieval-Sanskrit script that looked like labor workers or my children or both, my writing partners, survivors I had talked to along the way, my whole extended family, students, friends, relatives long gone whose voices live on in mine, the woman in the health food store, the man whose car I hit, friends I hadn't seen in years—we all had one singular voice to share. Even the man who sat on the park bench two and a half years before, his voice, too, was a part of mine; if only that day either of us had known what to listen for.

Retrogression 50:
July 1988.

I'm at a party in my early twenties, somewhat tipsy, with a woman from work and her friends. She introduces me to a man. He is tall, personable. We talk for over an hour and then he kisses me. I realize it's late, after eleven, and I had promised my parents I'd be home by 11:30 p.m. "I need to find Esther," I say. "I have to get home." "I'll drive you," he says. But once in his car, he drives in the opposite direction and then down a dirt road. "I need my license," he says. "I shouldn't be driving without it. It's just down the street at my house."

He arrives at a small, dark cottage. "I'll wait in the car," I tell him. "No, you're coming with me," he says as he opens my door and grabs my arm. We move through the night. He unlocks the house and pulls me in. He pushes me onto a bed and I struggle to get away from him. He pins my hands. Soon he's trying to have sex with me. "Please don't," I say. "Don't do this. I don't want to get pregnant. I need to be home. I'm not on birth control." I'm saying this over and over again and then something almost stops me from breathing. I have remembered bits and pieces of this childhood memory with the man, but suddenly I remember the whole story and this memory freezes me in place. I stop struggling and watch as things unfold, but I no longer feel a thing.

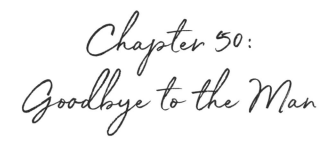

Chapter 50:
Goodbye to the Man

I go to Lara's house for lunch.

"I got an email from my cousin after she read something I wrote about her family. She's misunderstood. I've hurt her."

"Which story is it?" Lara asks. "I don't remember reading it."

"I took it out of the book. It actually isn't a good fit, but I wanted her to read it anyway. I thought it might bring us closer."

Lara sits with me on the couch.

"I can't do this anymore," I say. "I can't write these pieces."

"What does the email say?" Lara asks.

I read it out loud.

"Look, Christine. I'm not saying this email is good. It's not. But she's communicating here. She's telling you how she feels. Your story accomplished what you wanted. Write her back. Keep talking."

"Maybe I should be honest with her about why I am writing this book. Perhaps I need to tell her about the man," I say.

"Yes, if you want to really know her and understand her, she needs to understand you."

"But I can't tell her his name. I can't."

"Why?"

"What if my parents and brothers learn who this man really is? It would hurt them," I say.

"But it's hurt you all these years. They'll be okay."

"I know, but why cause unnecessary pain?"

Lara doesn't say a word. Neither do I. But for the first time, I hate the man who molested me—not for what he did to me physically, but for putting me in the position of having to tell the people I love something that will hurt them.

"But maybe they want to talk about it. Maybe it will be good for all of you to get this out."

"Maybe," I say.

"So why not?"

I take in a deep breath. "Because nobody will believe me."

I begin to cry.

"Nobody will believe me."

"Why wouldn't they?"

"Because I barely believe it myself."

Lara looks at me and I can tell she's trying to understand.

"This man was a wonderful man. There was nothing not to like about this man. He stood for so many things I love about this world. He made people happy."

"But he hurt you," she says. "He's not so wonderful after all."

We pause and I run through the exchange with my cousin in my head. The story about my cousin described how I had allowed a falling-out in junior high to affect the way I interacted with her even today. I was still afraid of being rejected by her, I had admitted to her in an email. But the more I think about it, the more I realize I'm afraid of being rejected by my entire family, not just this one cousin.

"Lara," I say. "If I tell my family about this and they don't believe me, they will reject me. That's what I've been afraid of all these years."

Later that evening, I change the man's name in my book to his real name. Maybe knowing the man's identity is key to my family understanding me today. Admitting to people I was molested had already made my life feel completely out of control. By keeping the story locked up and away from anybody else's consciousness, I had actually contained it. Yet, it had gained momentum behind that locked door.

After I change the name in my manuscript, my world is chaotic. I am Dorothy blowing through the skies in a house that has suddenly lost its foundation. For the next week, I wake in the middle of the night in a panic. After every meal I think I'm going to throw up. I can't take in enough air.

At work we have a visitor from Australia who is writing an article about our program. One afternoon Lara and I take him out for coffee. Andrew is young, light, fun, and I find myself forgetting my life's dramas, laughing out loud. At a certain point, Lara grabs a newspaper and begins to read our horoscopes. She reads Andrew's and it's all about reaching out to people, making new ties, allowing others to help him accomplish his goals. Then she reads mine. It has words like vacuum and vortex in it. It uses the word "swirling."

I'm in the car when it hits me. I'm thinking about a recent conversation I had with my father on the phone, one where I revealed I had been sexually abused, although I hadn't told him by whom.

"I want to tell you something so you will understand me better," I had said.

"But . . ." he had responded. "I love you. You don't need to explain anything to me."

I told him anyway.

But now I am considering moving beyond what I have told him, telling him the actual identity of the man, imagining he could never guess, even though he has been telling me all along he really doesn't want to hear. This time I replay his words to me, and I listen to them as they float through my car. *You don't need to explain anything. I understand. I love you. You don't have to explain.*

I relax my shoulders for the first time in over a week. Suddenly it's clear as day. My father already knows.

I go back to my manuscript and make a decision, one that ends the whirlwind that began a few weeks or perhaps even years before, and I change the man's name back to be just a man. I have one more note to write. I type my brothers' names: To George, Ernie, Milo, Zach. "I'm ready to send you a copy of my book," my email begins and I wait as one by one they email back saying they will read it.

Retrogression 51:
Sometime in the late seventies.

It's summertime and I'm visiting them. The man's wife is asleep in the next room. He's scratching my back and I'm sitting on his lap. I smell alcohol and there's a glass of yellow liquid with ice on the table next to his chair. Soon he's tickling me, first on the sides of my body and then in other places, closer and closer to my underwear, then in my underwear, underneath the material touching my rear end, then brushing over my breasts, although I know I didn't have breasts then. I keep laughing and pushing his hands away and he starts breathing heavy and moving my butt and crotch over a lump in his pants. He keeps moving me back and forth, back and forth. I have shorts on and a summer tank, but I still feel the lump and I'm sure this is something I shouldn't be feeling.

Chapter 51:
All the Silent Spaces

The thing I regret the most about our encounter is not what I did when you were there, but that I didn't hug my daughter right after you ran off. She was crying and saying "Mom" over and over again. But I was covered in blood and didn't want to scare her, so I turned away. Hadn't you already scared her enough? I wonder what message she took from this. That I didn't love her anymore? That I was ashamed of what had happened to us? A friend of mine told me this is my fault—that I'm too open to the world, too trusting, and she wasn't surprised this happened. **This is not my fault.** Do you know what it means that I can't trust you anymore? Everything.

I have been at Eliza's house since 7:00 p.m. reading passages of my book and now it's after midnight. For Eliza, something isn't adding up about the attack and it's showing itself in one piece, a letter I wrote to the attacker at the beginning of the book, my original preface. We have been looking at this piece for over an hour, and Eliza is convinced I need to change it. It's winter and as we talk, we drink Eliza's favorite tea from steamy mugs. I hold on to the sides, absorb the heat into my hands, and my whole body feels warm.

"There's something about this paragraph that's not working for me," Eliza says.

"I like it," I say. "And it's the only point in the first piece where I explore Ada's reaction to the crime. I want her there."

"But it doesn't ring true as far as what a little girl would think," Eliza says.

She looks at her dog, smiles, and then looks back at me, her expression again serious.

"Well, I'm imagining what she might have been thinking at the time," I say.

"But it's not written in a little girl's sensibility. I think you're putting some of your own feelings into Ada's reaction in this part. Ada wouldn't take these messages from you. That you don't love her anymore? Maybe she's more afraid and reacting to her fear. Maybe she's just trying to be comforted."

"I took the paragraph out months ago, but then I put it back," I acknowledge.

"See, that says it all. You don't feel it belongs there either," Eliza says, lifting her tea.

"Well, I took it out because you and Felix thought it didn't belong. But I really feel it's necessary—vital even. I can't explain why," I say.

"What bothers me is little girls don't analyze like you do here. That's not Ada's voice at all. Maybe it's yours, but if it is, it doesn't belong here. And this isn't written for your reader, either. It's for you."

"I think it belongs," I say.

Eliza leans forward, looks at the text with me, and points to the words "ashamed" and "fault."

"See, here it is. You're projecting some of your feelings onto Ada. She doesn't feel this way. You do."

I pause for a moment because what Eliza says causes a chain reaction. Bells ring, whistles go off everywhere in my head. I can hardly contain it.

Eliza puts down her mug and looks at me. "Christine, this little girl isn't Ada. This little girl is you."

I can feel my face flush.

I touch the page in front of us as if to make sure it's the same piece of paper we had been reading a moment before.

"I'm the little girl," I say and suddenly I feel, perhaps for the first time, the full weight of the violence I have experienced. Months earlier I had been looking for a support group for assault but could only find groups for domestic violence and rape. Why hadn't I seen it? Both these groups could have helped me.

"Christine, this was the first piece you ever wrote for this book. This has been here the whole time."

Eliza picks up a cracker and then puts it down again. She lifts the page of my book and holds it in front of her. She reads the paragraph again, silently, slowly. Then she looks at me.

"In bold letters you have, 'This is not my fault.' This is the only place in the book where you have something in bold."

The spell of this discovery lingers. There's something powerful in the air I have never felt before, something I can almost touch. That night I tell Eliza everything and for her something clicks, something she had perhaps already known, but couldn't put into words—the event in the parking lot was a catalyst for something else, something deeper; it was the start of an unpeeling of sorts.

That night something shifts for me, too. It occurs to me the world is filled with little girls. They are everywhere, in all the silent spaces. They're peeking into the doors of a million support groups nobody will go into. They're in parking lots, cellars, forests, cities, boardrooms, houses—those quiet places where they were molested, raped, attacked, hit, shut down, turned away, diminished, chastised, ignored. They are everywhere. Long before "Me Too" was a movement, they were saying these two words in silent exclamations. If only we had looked up from what we were doing, we would have seen their resounding presence.

Epilogue: Running Unafraid

When we arrive in Maine this year, something is different. It's July 2011, and a small bird is sitting on its eggs over the entrance to my parents' home. My mother opens the door when she sees our car and the bird shoots away from her eggs, fluttering above until long after the door has closed behind us. We watch from windows as she finally floats back to the nest and settles in. We spend hours watching the bird. She circles nearby when we're outside. We wonder if her babies will ever hatch. Can they survive these summer afternoons while their mother flutters above them?

Within forty-eight hours, my legs ache for a run. In Atlanta I have two running partners, Betty and Georgia. Betty and I talk about everything—her parents, her recovery from cancer, my children, our inevitable ups and downs. Georgia has long runner's legs and I struggle to keep up. During the three-mile trek through town, I never think I'll make it, but somehow I do. Before my trip, Georgia asks if I will run alone in Maine.

"I don't run alone," I admit. "I stick close to my parents' house and usually Sam comes with me. He bolts ahead but then gets tired. I have to carry him home."

"Has this been since the attack?" Georgia asks.

"No, I've always been afraid to run alone. The attack just made it worse."

But the idea of running alone has been growing in me since our conversation and I decide to try it. The paths I take on dirt roads are beautiful—long, winding, deserted. During the first twenty minutes, I spend most of my time imagining escape routes—what will I do if a man grabs me by the shoulders? I will run toward the water and swim away. I'll try to remember an aikido move or one of the karate maneuvers my son recently taught me. I'll rip off pieces of clothing to leave as clues for the police. This third idea distracts me for a moment. I think of Elie Wiesel's *Night* and the description of his ghetto after everyone had been shot to death or put on trains during the Holocaust; traces of families and lives strewn over empty streets—evidence.

I've been listening to books on tape about the Holocaust—Elie Wiesel, Anne Frank, a number of other nonfiction writers who chronicle life during the Second World War. I've learned about rebel fighters, the underground movements to save Jews, ghettos, death marches, concentration camp survival stories. I want answers from these books. What separates the living from the dead, the survivors from those who perished? Do they hold on to some secret? And how did camp survivors go on, live sanely, without fear?

As I run, I replay a memory I have of Livio Valentini, an Italian artist from Orvieto. In 2001, during the Spoleto Festival in Charleston, South Carolina, he displayed his work for thousands of people to view. I was in my early thirties, teaching at a local college. During the weekend of the festival, I was his interpreter. The organizers sent us on a horse and carriage ride. Valentini had survived Buchenwald, and his art was filled with haunting caged birds. During our carriage ride, Valentini drew people pulling a carriage with horses standing on top of it. "What a beautiful horse ride," he said to me and showed me the picture.

All weekend my conversation with Valentini was light and fun. We shared secret jokes in Italian. In receiving lines, Valentini turned to me and fabricated stories about each person. "He's the Archduke of Salami. She just found out her husband smokes lima beans. This man recently joined the circus."

One evening we walked through the center of Charleston with a group of people. The air was fragrant and warm. As we walked, Valentini kept slowing his pace. I slowed mine too, content to be outside and in the moment of a conversation. It would take a few minutes for the rest of the group to notice.

"Stay here with me," he said as they receded from view one time. "You make me feel younger. I don't want to talk about the serious things they discuss. I'd prefer to play this game of hide-and-seek with them."

At my parents' house, my father and I have the same discussions we do every year about locking doors at night, making sure the chicken is cooked through, fire hazards. He still gestures and throws his arms into the air, telling me how safe Maine is and threatening to give me burnt chicken for dinner, but something has changed. I'm no longer embarrassed or ashamed to speak up.

By the end of our first week in Maine, the bird sits uninterrupted on her nest in the midst of our traffic. She looks down, daring us to bother her, and then one day, we hear tiny chirps.

I run up and down hills at a comfortable stride. I look at the water, the trees, and I realize I'm running at my own pace, without pain. The lake stretches away from the dirt road, and when I turn the corner, all I can smell is an earthly peace, a calm quiet. The anxieties I have been playing hide-and-seek with all year seem far away.

I pick up my pace and soon I am running faster than I have ever run before, and I can't think of anything but my lungs as they fill with air, running unafraid through the forest.

Afterword: Atrophy

Eleven years after I was attacked in front of my children in a parking lot, thirty years after I had been raped in college, and forty-two years after I had been molested, I attended a four-person gathering at my Italian colleague's new house. I had just been to see my gynecologist and she had told me as a result of menopause, my vagina had atrophied. "Atrophied?" Lara asked. "Yes," I said. "It happens to all women after menopause." Two of my colleagues began to talk about Kegels, how I should do them. I disagreed. "This is a result of hormonal changes," I reminded them. "Besides, my doctor told me it was nothing to be concerned about. It happens to all women," I relayed. "The funniest part of the conversation, though, was what my doctor said afterward. She told me, 'Atrophy's a terrible word choice. I'm sure it was named that by a man.'"

My colleagues were surprised by my open discussion about atrophy, but I felt such relief at sharing news that didn't involve my daughter, who, at sixteen, was out of school suffering from anxiety and depression. Unfortunately, we already had experience in this field. Sam had developed anxiety-induced seizures resulting in a lost year of doctors' appointments and missed school. My children had grown up to be deep thinkers, activists, caring out-of-the-box problem solvers, sensitive, beautiful, loving teens, but often they were without skin, completely open to the pain of the world.

When we brought Ada to a counselor, one of the first things she mentioned was the attack that had happened to us when she was five. "Thinking about that man makes me so angry. I wish I could go back in time and harm him just enough to stop him from hurting anyone." The counselor responded, "What you experienced, Ada, was trauma. Real trauma. It lives in your body now. We have to find a way to release some of the stress it has caused you." I wondered about Ada's depression and Sam's seizures. Was the memory of our trauma the root of their anxiety?

A week before Ada stopped going to school, I had been preoccupied and angry, outraged by the US Senate's reaction to superior court nominee Brett Kavanaugh's proceedings after a professor had accused him of sexual assault. When Christine Blasey Ford spoke about her attack, her words echoed how I had felt during my own college rape. How was it that a bunch of mostly old, white men, who had never experienced rape or assault, were to make this final decision? They said all the things women who experience assault hear over and over again. Why did it take her so long to report the assault? Why couldn't she remember where the assault took place? Why didn't anyone else at the party remember it? Was she doing this for fame, notoriety? How could such a decent man commit such an atrocity—it couldn't have been him. They apologized to Kavanaugh over and over again, in front of me, in front of a nation of assault survivors. And the US president mocked Ford at a rally and said every man should fear being falsely accused. How was it these men, so out of touch with survivors and women in general, had the power to put into office a man who could ultimately decide the future of so many issues affecting women?

I decided to return to counseling. At my appointment I told my counselor, an expert in trauma recovery, about my anger with the Kavanaugh hearing. I outlined what I had learned from writing my book. "What you have done is courageous," she said. "You took time to understand what you've been through, to look it straight in the eyes, analyze it, explain it to your family and to yourself. However, I don't think you've ever felt it."

Her words stung. They were true. Although I had cried about the man once in college, I had never allowed myself to examine how I felt, perhaps afraid of what I would find. But there was one time, not long ago, when, as I sat outside with my husband drinking wine, I talked about the man, how funny he was. I told stories—how he melted salt pork into his pasta e fagioli. "Don't strain it out," he had told me when I asked him for the recipe. I loved his pasta e fagioli and was willing to add a little unhealthy fat to my diet, so I kept the salt pork when I cooked this dish. And I remembered once, when I had shown him a photo from Christmas. The photo was of my brother holding up a new T-shirt. But I had snapped the picture from behind the couch and there, in the photo, on the back of the man's head, was a big bald spot in the center. My brothers and I were laughing like crazy when we showed him. He took the picture, a pen, and colored the spot in, right in front of us. As I talked about the man tears poured down my face.

Acknowledgments

I have begun this page so many times and I've finally come to the conclusion that the number of people who have helped me over the past twelve years is impossible to count. You have all made a difference. So many people shared a smile when I needed one. Some of you were there with me in the trenches every day. Many of you appear in my stories. I have received donations, kind words, fearless listening, tears, love. For those of you who read my chapters and provided feedback, thank you. You moved this book forward. To those who donated to my book's publication, thank you. Without you I would not be reaching this milestone. To those of you who challenged my ideas, asked me difficult questions, and helped me move forward, thank you. You guided me toward understanding some of life's greatest mysteries, some personal, some profound and universal. To the many who sent encouraging letters, emails, texts, cards, messages, and words, and bore witness to my story, thank you. You kept me going. To the colleagues, friends, and students who invited me to speak on the topic of women and violence, thank you. You helped me be there for others. To my family, thank you for holding me up during difficult times. To my students and children, thank you for teaching me how to be vulnerable, alive, and a part of this world. To Word Creative Literary Services and Emory's Center for Faculty Development and Excellence, thank you for your encouragement, you helped me believe in my work. To my publisher, She Writes Press, thank you for so many reasons! You make dreams happen! It has been a twelve-year collective journey and during those years I have grown into the person I have always wanted to be. And you were all a part of it. For me, you have made all the difference.

About the Author

Christine Ristaino teaches Italian and is the faculty advisor for a number of programs related to social justice at Emory University. She has coauthored an academic publication titled *Lucrezia Marinella and the "Querelle des Femmes" in Seventeenth-Century Italy* and the first edition of a book series, *The Italian Virtual Class*. Ristaino specializes in Italian language pedagogy, language teaching, cultural acquisition, community engaged learning, and Italian memoir. She writes and publishes articles and op-eds on overcoming violence, having difficult conversations, and equity.

Author photo © Annemie Tonken